Euripides: Trojan Women

DUCKWORTH COMPANIONS
TO GREEK AND ROMAN TRAGEDY
Series editor: Thomas Harrison

DUCKWORTH COMPANIONS
TO GREEK AND ROMAN TRAGEDY

Euripides:
Trojan Women

Barbara Goff

Duckworth

First published in 2009 by
Gerald Duckworth & Co. Ltd.
90-93 Cowcross Street, London EC1M 6BF
Tel: 020 7490 7300
Fax: 020 7490 0080
info@duckworth-publishers.co.uk
www.ducknet.co.uk

A catalogue record for this book is available
from the British Library

ISBN 978 0 7156 3545 2

Typeset by Ray Davies
Printed and bound in Great Britain by
CPI Antony Rowe, Chippenham, Wiltshire

Contents

Contents

Acknowledgements

I would like to thank Tom Harrison, who invited me to write this book, and Deborah Blake of Duckworth, who has once again proved herself a model editor. I would like here to acknowledge also my abiding debts to family, friends, colleagues and students; and to honour in particular the staff of the Joint Library/Institute of Classical Studies Library, Senate House, London, who do an excellent job in sometimes difficult circumstances.

1

Contexts

'What's Hecuba to him, or he to Hecuba?'[1]

Euripides' *Trojan Women* has regularly been acclaimed as a drama of extraordinary power in depicting the sorrows of war. For some, the focus on war has seemed excessive; the play has often been dismissed as 'one long lament'.[2] Others, particularly in more recent years, have sensed that the play's figuring of war's devastation – the loss of homes, families, hope – addresses with disturbing precision their own struggles. The play provokes strong reactions.

Trojan Women is interested in much else besides lamentation. The quotation above from *Hamlet*, centring on Hekabe, the fallen queen of Troy, suggests that part of its fascination lies in the complex sympathy between those on stage and those who spectate. *Trojan Women* invites us both to identify with its characters and to stand back and judge them – and in the process to judge ourselves. A more recent response than that of Hamlet, Mary Renault's fictional account of a fourth-century BCE performance of *Trojan Women*, evokes both the play's power to move the audience and its self-awareness. Caught between the play's emotions and his professional responsibilities, the actor playing a dead child speaks: [3]

> Soon after came my cue to be brought on, dead ... The chorus called out the dreadful news to my grannie Hekabe; lying, eyes shut ... I prayed Dionysos not to let me sneeze. There was a pause which because I could not see seemed to last for ever. The whole theatre had got dead silent,

9

holding its breath. Then a terrible low voice said just beside me,
   Lay down the circled shield of Hektor on the ground.
... the voice seemed to go all through me, making my backbone creep with cold. I forgot it was I who was being mourned for. ... All I remember for certain is my swelling throat, and the horror that came over me when I knew I was going to cry.

My eyes were burning. Terror was added to my grief. I was going to wreck the play. The sponsor would lose the prize; Kroisos the crown; my father would never get a part again; we would be in the streets begging our bread. And after the play, I would have to face terrible Hekabe without a mask. Tears burst from my shut eyes; my nose was running. I hoped I might die, that the earth would open or the skene catch fire, before I sobbed aloud.

The hand that had traced my painted wounds lifted me gently. I was gathered into the arms of Hekabe; the wrinkled mask with its down-turned mouth bent close above. The flute, which had been moaning softly through the speech, getting a cue, wailed louder. Under its sound, Queen Hekabe whispered in my ear, 'Be quiet, you little bastard. You're dead.'

The power of the drama viscerally to move the audience is lovingly celebrated here, but the episode has it both ways, because it is voiced by the actor who shares responsibility for producing the illusion. He too is overcome, but if he does not maintain the illusion, he will likely be dead for real. In line with the concerns of my opening quotations, then, this book will foreground not only the emotional power of *Trojan Women*, but also its self-consciousness and intellectual energy.[4] I shall resist the hoary typing of the play as 'static', 'passive', or 'one long lament', by drawing attention to its dynamic structure, and by examining its capacity to generate new versions of itself in the twentieth century and beyond. My strategy will be to set the play in its historical and cultural context, before proceeding to

10

a close reading that allows a full appreciation of its dramatic development, and finally to an account of twentieth-century receptions. Before we embark on these investigations, however, we might review the overall claims that the play makes on our attention; what's Hecuba to us?

What's Hecuba to us?

Trojan Women is a play set in the immediate aftermath of the legendary defeat of Troy by the Greek army, and the women of the title are captives who spend the drama waiting to be assigned as slaves to their new masters. A brief initial scene between two gods, Poseidon and Athena, offers the possibility that the Greeks will also suffer in their turn, but the focus is otherwise firmly on the waiting women. Hardly anything happens except, precisely, waiting – at the end of the play the women leave for the Greek ships as Troy is put to the flames, but up till then, there is little that might count as 'action'. Numerous critics have accordingly complained that this drama is nothing like whatever tragedy is supposed to be; there are no heroes, no ghastly errors of judgement, no terrifying realisations or reversals. Instead, the logical consequences of the fall of Troy work themselves out in a series of scenes that pit the women, especially the erstwhile queen of Troy, Hekabe, against the consequences of the various dispositions made by the victorious Greeks.

The will of the conquerors is made known to the women by the Greek herald Talthybios, who announces their destinations. Thus, Hekabe's daughter Kassandra enters on her way to Agamemnon's ship, bound for a brief life and a shameful death as his concubine. The widow of Hekabe's son Hektor, Andromache, enters on her way to becoming the prize of Neoptolemos, son of the Greek warrior Achilles who killed Hektor. She tells Hekabe that another daughter, Polyxena, has been sacrificed at the tomb of Achilles, and learns herself that her son Astyanax, as heir to Hektor, is to be hurled to his death from the walls of Troy. Lastly there enters Helen, the woman, as all antiquity knew, who caused the Trojan War by leaving her Greek husband Menelaos and running away to Troy with Hekabe's son Paris. She comes to discover what Menelaos has decided to do with her – the answer is, to take her home – and incidentally to engage in a long debate with Hekabe about the causes of the Trojan War. Once these three 'daughters' of Hekabe have departed for their various fates, the final entrance is that of the child Astyanax, dead, and carried on his father Hektor's shield. The mourning for him by Hekabe and the Trojan women of the chorus modulates into the last lament for the burning city.

Trojan Women attained enough popularity to rank among the plays of Euripides most frequently copied out in antiquity, and in late antiquity it achieved 'canonical' status as one of the plays chosen to represent the author in schools.[5] On its first performance, however, in 415 BCE,[6] *Trojan Women* and the plays presented with it won second prize, runner up to a play by the now forgotten Xenocles, as Aelian 2.8 records. Lattimore remarks appositely that 'Aelian seems outraged that Euripides should come second; I can hardly understand how the Athenians let him present this play at all'.[7] Not only do readers wonder how the Athenians could have endured the play's searing indictment of warmongering, but they also criticise *Trojan Women* for various technical failings. The accusation is repeatedly levelled that *Trojan Women* is not a tragedy, or even not a good play; it has several defects of structure, and its overwhelming emotional effect constitutes a defect in taste.[8] The pronouncement of Gilbert Murray, who was a great champion of the play, sums up this strand of the criticism: 'Judged by common standards, the *Troades* is far from a perfect play; it is scarcely even a good play ... little plot, little construction, little or no relief or variety ... scene after scene passes beyond the due limits of the tragic art'.[9] Even critics who have no reservations about the play's quality have to agree that it presents other kinds of problems. Judith Mossman observes that the play is 'remarkably difficult to fit into many schemas that seek to formulate a definition for tragedy' and cites André Rivier to the effect that it cannot be a

12

tragedy because it consists of lamentation without reflection.[10] A related perception, repeated in the criticism, is that the play is static, episodic and without development; the most interesting version of this view is the work of Francis Dunn on *Trojan Women* as a play that cannot happen.[11]

While the chorus of disapproval clearly registers something disturbing and difficult about the play, it is contradicted by the contemporary popularity of *Trojan Women* in performance. Karelisa Hartigan draws this contrast explicitly: 'although some scholarly analysis of the drama tends to find it rather lacking in theme and characterization, it usually plays to a receptive audience'.[12] This popularity she attributes to the force of the play as an account of war: 'From the day when Euripides penned it in 415 BCE to the present time the suffering he portrayed of war's innocent victims has spoken to audiences in nearly every decade of the past century, for the pain of military conflict is apparently never ending'.[13] We shall consider the issue of the play's anti-war credentials subsequently, but note for now that this divergence between the experience of the play as text and as performance can be seen as a significant indicator of the new relations to Greek tragedy being worked out by the late twentieth and early twenty-first century. The issue is perhaps not a simple opposition between 'page' and 'stage', so much as a temporal disjunction whereby the second half of the twentieth century rediscovered the power of Greek tragedy as much through performance as through translations and texts.[14]

We should note also that the charges of excessive emotionalism, and of lack of movement or development, might amount to a charge of being female, and might thus register a resistance to the overwhelmingly female voice of the play.[15] Such a resistance could be characteristic of the early twentieth century but would have much less cultural purchase in more recent times, when, as Edith Hall shows, the prominence of women in Greek tragedy is one of the aspects that have secured it a very high profile in translation and adaptation.[16] Further fostering the elevation of *Trojan Women* in particular is the perception that military conflicts postdating World War II are often morally much more equivocal than was that mid-century combat, explicitly involving civilians as targets, and thus can readily be delivered to the play's searching gaze. *Trojan Women* speaks to modern audiences and readers not only about war, or women, but also about contemporary relationships to the tragic dramas of the Greeks.

Even without its recent prominence in performance, *Trojan Women* is astonishing enough, both in itself and in comparison with other Greek tragedies. For a start, although the play rarely figures prominently in feminist analyses of Greek drama, all the major characters are women. The only males are Astyanax, who is not a speaking part, Menelaos, whose one scene hardly shows him off to advantage, and Talthybios. Apart from these latter two, and their attendant soldiers, the Greeks are kept offstage and away from our view. In this they are not unlike the anonymous, usually menacing crowd that gathers offstage in other Euripidean dramas such as *Iphigeneia at Aulis* or *Orestes*, but in *Trojan Women* the Greeks are not only the nameless masses but also constitute the sole locus of power. The women on stage are victims, without even the victims' revenge such as characterises another Euripidean play set in the aftermath of the fall of Troy, *Hekabe*. Another salient difference from *Hekabe* that sheds light on *Trojan Women* is that the former takes place in an interstice of time after the war when the Greek fleet is becalmed; none of the actions was meant to happen, whereas the actions of *Trojan Women* are organised. Any possible departure from the Greeks' orderly plans – the mass suicide of the Trojan women, Kassandra setting fire to the tents (299-301), Andromache cursing her new masters (733-4), Hekabe throwing herself into the flames of the dying city (1282-3) – is prevented. The only thing that might count as a departure from proper procedure is that the captive women do all the talking.

In that the women do talk, this history, against all expectation, is told by the victims, with whom the audience or readers are consequently invited to identify – even though these victims are barbarians as well, and describe themselves as such.[17] The fraught nature of this identification is the object of much critical thought regarding the play, as well as of Hamlet's question with which we began.[18] It will occupy us at several different points in our analysis, particularly since it also relates to the Aristotelian account of tragic emotions as dependent on certain kinds of balances between self and other. In its orchestration of this difficult identification *Trojan Women* may be thought to recall Aeschylus' *Persians*, which was staged a few years after the Greeks defeated the Persian invasion, yet is set at the court of the vanquished Xerxes and populated entirely by grieving Persians. While *Persians*, the earlier play, is usually found to extend some sympathy to the failed tyrant Xerxes, there is no corresponding vilification of the Greeks, who are instead reluctantly celebrated by their defeated enemies.[19] In *Trojan Women*, while we are invited to identify with the losers, we are also invited to judge, and condemn, the victors. Various speakers seek to persuade us that the Greeks are barbarous, and even that the barbarians are Greek. Yet there is no easy polarisation either between bad Greeks and good Trojans, since we are also invited to subscribe to the more difficult hypothesis that Hekabe, not Helen, was responsible for the start of the Trojan War.

If we briefly pursue this forensic line of enquiry, we may recollect that the point of the human sympathy orchestrated by Hamlet's theatre was to find out the guilt of the king. A similar dynamic is at work in an early account of audience reaction to *Trojan Women*. The fourth-century tyrant Alexander of Pherae, renowned for devising inventive executions for his enemies, had to leave the theatre, 'because he was ashamed that the citizens could see him, who had never pitied any man that he had murdered, weeping over the sufferings of Hekabe and Andromache' (Plutarch *Pelopidas* 29. 4-6).[20] Not only are the representations of pitiful events devastating to the onlooker, but so also is the dissection of guilt and innocence undertaken by the drama. The notion that Hekabe may be responsible for the Trojan War is an indication that guilt and innocence become hard to distinguish, and *Trojan Women* proceeds also to suggest

15

that defeat and victory themselves are not very different from each other, or indeed may have changed places. Consequently, we may eventually discover that our identification must be with the deadly Greeks as much as with the suffering Trojans. It is this dialectic of victory and defeat, and guilt and innocence, as much as the representation of loss and misery attendant on conflict, which has made the play repeatedly invoked as an anti-war statement.

In this book I shall endeavour to give weight to a reading of the play in its late fifth-century context, and to this end I shall first discuss contemporary Athenian politics and culture, before considering theatrical practice and the development of tragedy as a genre. The latter discussion will include an account of the trilogy to which *Trojan Women* apparently belonged. After these preliminary considerations, my approach to the play itself will be by a continuous close reading rather than a thematic analysis, countering the charge of static immobility with an emphasis on the pace and dynamism of the play as it unfolds. Within this framework certain themes and issues will emerge repeatedly, chief among them the question of the identity of victory and defeat; other preoccupations will include the relations between gods and mortals, between men and women, Greek and barbarian, and language and the world. A further issue will be how the play has frequently polarised the responses of readers and audiences, between nihilistic despair and a determination to retrieve from the ruins some spark of consolation. From this reading of the play we move in the last part of this study to an account of some elements of its twentieth-century reception. As Hall and Macintosh show, *Trojan Women* has hardly any reception history until the twentieth century, when it becomes exceptionally compelling to writers and theatre practitioners alike.[21] Seneca's *Troades* can, of course, be considered an early reception of the Euripidean play, but I have not dealt with Seneca's *Troades* in this book, partly for reasons of space, but primarily because it deserves a Companion to itself.

1. Contexts

Athens in 415

Trojan Women was first performed at the City Dionysia in 415, when the crucial characteristics of the polis of Athens include that it is a mature, radical democracy, and that it is at war with the polis of Sparta. Both these considerations require further discussion. To take the war first: together responsible for driving a deadly Persian invasion out of Greece in the early years of the fifth century, Athens and Sparta had since pursued different lines of political and military development until mutual wariness escalated into conflict. The Peloponnesian War, named after the Peloponnese where the most powerful polis was the oligarchic Sparta, began in 431 and did not end until the defeat of Athens in 404. 415 falls in a curious hiatus called the 'Peace of Nikias' during which the major players, Athens and Sparta, did not fight one another but were distracted with other adventures. Chief among these at Athens were the conquest of the island of Melos in 416, with ensuing executions of men and enslavement of women and children, and the plan to invade Sicily, which got underway in 415 itself.

We are remarkably well informed about the Peloponnesian War, which pitted Greek against Greek in a way that was troubling even to contemporaries, because it was recorded almost in real time by the Athenian writer Thucydides. His *History* is renowned not only for the battle narratives and details of strategy, but for those elements which make it a meditation, on war and on the exercise of power in wartime, as much as it is a record. Such elements include speeches by the major politicians and generals, which punctuate the narrative, and also excursuses on the moral dimensions of the conflict, such as those which describe the plague in Athens of 430 (2.47-55) and the civil strife at Corcyra in 427 (3.82-3). In excursuses like these, the descriptions encourage the conclusion that the war led to a breakdown in traditional morality and even in traditional notions of language and communication. Such conclusions have often seemed very relevant to an understanding of tragedy, and we shall revisit them shortly.

17

If we move now to consider the other characteristic of late fifth-century Athens, its mature radical democracy, we can explain the 'maturity' by the fact that the polis had been used to governing itself more or less democratically for nearly 100 years.[22] 'Democracy' in this context is participatory rather than representative; the Assembly of all citizens (free adult males) was responsible for almost all decisions on the running of the polis both internally and in its relationships with other cities, and the mechanisms of democracy had developed to cope with many eventualities – though arguably not all. Why the democracy is also termed 'radical' is because by 415, almost all the offices of the polis were awarded by lot, ensuring wide participation by men from all classes and statuses. This had not always been the case. In the early days of democracy the traditional noble families continued to supply the most prominent politicians, and even the democratic revolution itself was spearheaded by a member of the powerful and aristocratic Alkmaeonid family, Kleisthenes. Perikles, perhaps the fifth century's most important politician, was also related to the Alkmaeonids, and his sway over the Assembly, from the 460s until 429 when he died of the plague, was sometimes likened to a particularly benign monarchy.[23]

Our view of the developments in the democracy after the traditional noble families lost their grip is conditioned by the nature of our sources, most of which derive from the aristocratic level of society.[24] After the death of Perikles, the conventional story runs, practical control of Athens fell to men who did not understand where Athens' true interests lay; of low social origin, they did not have Perikles' education or experience. Labelled 'demagogues' by sources such as Thucydides and Aristophanes, with connotations of corruption and populist opportunism, politicians like Kleon and Hyperbolos were in fact wealthy and educated, even if not perhaps in the traditional ways, and their policies were intelligible, even if not precisely Periklean.[25] Their prominence in the democracy, however, marking a felt departure from the Periklean paradigm, contributes to the impression of social confusion and breakdown.

1. Contexts

As with the war's assault on morality, so with the processes of democracy and demagoguery; Thucydides' *History* provides the most memorable account, and on a topic that will prove germane to our discussions of *Trojan Women*. In Book 3 occurs the Mytilinean Debate, concerning a suitable punishment for an island ally who had revolted in 427. This Debate has long been held to show the Athenian democracy at its worst, or at least its most stressed, since on one day the Assembly decided to execute the males and sell off the women and children, but on the next day had a change of heart and revoked its own decision. The sailors who bore the second message, of reprieve, were paid extra wages to row extra fast and overtake the first, doomladen ship. During the debate Kleon is portrayed as 'the most violent, and the most persuasive' (3.36) of contemporary speakers, arguing that the self-interest of an imperial power demands ruthlessness. 'You do not see that your rule is a tyranny, over subjects who are unwilling and who plot against you. They obey you not because you might indulge them, to your own injury, and not because of their good will, but because you are superior to them in strength' (3.37). His opponent Diodotos makes none of the expected appeals to humanity, but contends instead that precisely the same self-interest requires that democracies spare the common people and punish only the (aristocratic) ring-leaders. To discuss the fate of doomed cities, then, is a thinkable element of public policy in fifth-century Athens, and the complex contours of self-interest are not unfamiliar. This discourse clearly feeds into the debates of *Trojan Women*. An even closer possible connection between *Trojan Women* and contemporary Athenian politics will be examined later on.

The kind of language that Kleon and Diodotos use, and indeed that Thucydides uses, is conditioned above all by the intellectual enquiries generated in Athens through the activity of the sophists. The sophists are perhaps a third element which we should highlight as part of what constitutes fifth-century Athens. As with the 'demagogues', our chief source for sophistic activity, namely Plato, is hostile, and the comedies of Aristophanes are also very dubious about its worth. To define the sophists and sophistic activity is difficult except in a crude ostensive way, but we can say that they constitute a philosophical dimension to the general social upheaval of the fifth century. With increased commercial, political and artistic activity went an unprecedented interrogation of traditional habits of thought and action. Reliance on human endeavour in the fields of, for instance, medicine and seamanship, and the relative success of that endeavour, meant that earlier notions of divinity came in for renewed scrutiny; reliance on human decision-making in the processes of democracy led to investigation of human motives and of the power of persuasive language. Sophists took this kind of enquiry as their task, and their conclusions necessarily troubled the traditional outlook.

Originating in several cities, the men known collectively as the sophists were migrant intellectuals who settled disproportionately in Athens, presumably because of its democratic openness and tolerance of debate – which they managed to stretch to its limits and sometimes beyond.[26] Protagoras, for instance, asserted that 'the human being is the measure of all things', which might seem in many contexts an overweening claim; Gorgias is responsible for the formulation that 'nothing exists; if it did, we could not know it; if we could know it, we could not communicate our knowledge' – a sentiment as alarming to the fifth century BCE as it proved to be to the twentieth century CE when Derrida promulgated not dissimilar views.[27] Wherever they were, sophists taught, and they collected audiences especially of young men, who were eager to question received wisdom. What they claimed to teach, among other philosophical topics, often included '*aretê*', which is usually translated in English by 'virtue'. '*Aretê*' is usually more colourful than 'virtue' and has a greater sense of masculine striving; 'excellence' is another common translation, but 'success' might be a possibility too. 'Success' in the fifth-century Athenian context implied power within and even over the Assembly, so the sophists often taught the means of persuasive language that would win a debate, and came to be identified with the

20

power of language to achieve mastery over one's fellow-citizens, whether for their good or not. It is this development that brought the sophists the most censure, and the common charge that they made the 'worse' (less virtuous) argument into the 'better' (more successful).[28] The many sources from fifth-century Athens that display concern about language and its manipulation speak compellingly of the anxieties of a society used to conducting its business through the medium of public speech.

Tragedy in 415

The war, the new political developments, and the radically questioning philosophical activity of the sophists, with their accompanying changes and types of breakdown, all placed Athens in 415, and indeed much of late fifth-century Greece, under considerable stress. While such stress is legible in tragedy, the genre is also conditioned by other factors important for our account of *Trojan Women*. Although we have complete plays by only three dramatists, and of those dramatists only a small proportion of their oeuvre, we have enough other information to indicate the general condition of the theatrical tradition within which *Trojan Women* was produced. Tragedy in 415, like democracy, is both mature and radical. Roughly the same age as democracy, tragedy is possibly closely linked with it at its inception.[29] There are good arguments which claim that Dionysos, as a god presiding over community events and communal identification, was an obvious choice for a democracy to celebrate, and indeed the dramatic performances developed as part of the major festival of Dionysos, the City Dionysia.[30] The genre also exhibits affinities to democratic, or at least civic, practice in its formal dimensions. With an audience of fifteen thousand – roughly three times the size of the Athenian assembly – tragedy at the Dionysia was a mass event. Seating may well have been by tribe, and judges were drawn from tribes, so that all the polis was represented. The chief elected officials of the democracy, the generals or *stratêgoi*, also had a prominent role in the proceedings.[31] Tragedy's discursive content has also often been linked to the workings of fifth-century democracy, since it partakes of the plurality of competing voices characteristic of the Athenian system, and displays an active questioning stance towards conventional pieties.[32]

Tragedy in 415 is 'mature' because it has developed considerably over a relatively short span. Although its 'original' form is unknown, scholars find it plausible that there was first a chorus, and then that a protagonist detached himself from the chorus to engage it in dialogue.[33] (A protagonist was always 'himself', because tragedies were written, produced and acted exclusively by men.) Several tragedies have scenes of debate between protagonist and chorus, although *Trojan Women* does not. The conventional narrative has it that Aeschylus added one more actor and Sophocles a third, after which no more were added, so that the majority of tragedies have two and three person scenes with interventions by the chorus, divided by longer sung passages ('choral odes') from the chorus. Where there are more than three roles to play, the actors must double up. In contrast, in *Trojan Women* the protagonist or first actor is on stage the whole time, playing Hekabe, which is an unusual and demanding situation.[34] The deuteragonist or second actor presumably took the parts of Kassandra, Andromache and Helen in turn, leaving the tritagonist (third actor) to play Talthybios and Menelaos.

Other theatrical choices made by the play are as notable as the unrelieved stage presence of Hekabe. By the time of *Trojan Women*, scene-painting, the invention of which is credited to Sophocles, had become a regular component of the dramatic *mîse en scène*; so indeed had the *skênê*, the building behind the stage, which in many plays functions almost as another character, and is certainly like a part of the plot. There is much less obvious call for scene-painting in *Trojan Women* than in for instance *Ion*, with its descriptions of the temple at Delphi, and the *skênê*-building, which represents the tents of the Greek commanders where the women are held, is much less of a tangible presence than for instance the house of Theseus and

Phaidra in *Hippolytos*. Nor does *Trojan Women* call upon theatrical devices like the *ekkuklêma* or the *mêchanê*. The *ekkuklêma* is a rolling platform that comes out of the *skênê*-building on to the stage, in order to display a scene that would otherwise be interior; the *mêchanê* is a kind of crane which brings a god or other special being flying on to the stage at roof height. The absence of these devices means that there is no epiphany by a *deus ex machina*, a 'god from the machine', to close the play, nor is there any violent act done off stage in the building whose consequences are then displayed outside. The violence is almost all over and done with before the play begins, except for the death of Astyanax, which happens on the city walls. Nor is this one act of violence reported in a messenger speech, which is an even more notable absence than others, since the messenger with the story of disaster from an offstage location is a regular feature of tragedy.[35] So despite the wealth of dramatic and theatrical procedures that were available to 'mature' tragedy, *Trojan Women* avails itself of none. Its poverty of device is like the destitution of the women themselves, throwing the play on the resources of the actors in the rhythms of song, speech, and orchestrated action.

Tragedy was also 'mature' in 415 in that it was highly self-conscious. Even though plays were only performed once at the City Dionysia, they passed into cultural memory by other means, as we can deduce from the fact that the comedies of Aristophanes make frequent references to plays that had been staged years earlier.[36] Whole scenes in some comedies depend on very specific parodies of tragedy, and tragedies were also highly aware of other tragedies. Especially after the decree (dated to the last third of the fifth century) which committed the polis to funding any new production of a tragedy which had first been staged by Aeschylus,[37] new tragedies can often be seen to grapple with the authority of the earlier plays.[38] There were other means to prolong the life of an apparently ephemeral drama. Tragedies might be performed at rural Dionysia after their premieres at the City festival, and they might also be read in Athens' (never very extensive) book trade. Memorisation of tragic songs and speeches was also a feature of Athenian culture. Tragic quotations appear in fourth century legal speeches,[39] and tragedy is alleged to have saved lives in even more desperate situations. When the Spartans finally defeated Athens in 404, they planned to raze the city to the ground, but were dissuaded from this course of action, the story goes, by a man from Phocis singing the first choral ode from Euripides' *Elektra*. And before the end of the war, when the Athenian navy was destroyed in Sicily, some of the men enslaved and dying in the Syracusan quarries allegedly gained their freedom by singing the latest choral poems from Euripides (Plutarch *Lysander* 15.3, *Nicias* 29.2).

What encourages extensive memorisation, parody and similar re-productions of tragedy is the fact that it is highly stylised, conventional and non-naturalistic. In such a structured genre, any formal innovations can be startling and significant, so that the 'mature' and 'radical' aspects of the genre can be seen to be interdependent. The dramaturgy of Euripides is noted for its destabilising of generic and formal expectations, accompanied by an extreme version of the radical questioning that we have attributed above to tragedy, and indeed to fifth-century discourse in general. Euripides' dramas have always been perceived as the most iconoclastic and disturbing of those we possess, and we can read this perception even in antiquity in the plays of Aristophanes.[40] In one respect, however, tragedy did not innovate at all, and that is in the matter of plot. As Aristotle remarks in his *Poetics* (1453a) the corpus of tragedy quickly settled on a restricted repertoire of plots drawn from panhellenic mythology; the best tragedies were all drawn from the fates of a handful of doomed families. While it was not until Agathon's work, in the fourth century, that entirely new plots for tragedy were devised (*Poetics* 1451b20-3), another possible source of plot, namely contemporary history, was also rejected. Of the extant tragedies only Aeschylus' *Persians* makes overt reference to the lived experience of his audience, and in earlier years such reference had been explicitly discouraged. When Phrynichos in the late 490s produced *The Fall of Miletus*, an event in the history of Greek relations with the Persian empire that had taken place in 494, the audience was so devastated with grief for the fate of the Milesians, who were Ionian Greeks and hence related to Athenians, that the play was banned and the dramatist fined (Herodotus 6.21). Subsequent writers learned quickly, and almost all the contemporary references that can be read in extant tragedy are heavily coded as mythical discourse. We shall, as noted, consider in a subsequent section the possibility of contemporary reference in *Trojan Women*.

'Mythical discourse' for fifth-century Greeks meant Homeric epic, the cultural authority of which was unparalleled. While the Homeric *Iliad* takes as its subject the war at Troy, it ends before the city does and instead, envisages that end in the words of Trojans who fear it. Thus in Book 6 Andromache foretells her own and her son's sufferings when Hektor will have died, and in 24 even imagines that son's death on the walls, whereas Hektor in 6 tries to turn her lamentation around by envisaging him as an avenging adult. We shall see later on how these moments are replayed in *Trojan Women*.[41] While the relation to Homeric epic thus has a formal dimension, in language and plot, critics also agree that tragedy in general stages multiple ideological collisions between the values promulgated in epic and those of fifth-century democracy. Thus the dramas repeatedly confront individual masculine heroism and martial glory with the necessity of more collective, social priorities.[42] In respect of this ideological formation, *Trojan Women* reaches for the extremes; there is no functioning society left, but the heroic ethos is also rejected out of hand. Although the play returns to the most recognisably Homeric, heroic, epic territory for its subject matter, it deprives its male characters of any glory or renown, instead exposing them as craven thugs. The only stably heroic figure is Hektor, who is not only dead, but whose absence is physically imaged forth in the shield that bears his son's body.

Trojan Women makes other extreme moves. Few other extant plays have the demand on the protagonist that he be present throughout the entire stage time, or the relentlessly episodic structure that has 'no parallel in serious drama'.[43]

25

Precisely these aspects have led to the criticism that the play is 'static'. No other extant play is set at the fall of a city; although plenty of tragic cities may be under threat, none of them, not even Aeschylus' Persepolis, is about to be wiped off the map as is Euripides' Troy. The play is exceptional in other ways too: it has, as mentioned above, no messenger speech; it has the largest number of half-line exchanges in the extant corpus (called 'half-stichomythia'); it is the only extant play to end on a lyric, sung exchange and in lyric metre rather than the iambic metre that represents dramatic speech.[44] It also forms part, the last part, of what may have been a fairly innovative trilogy, which we should briefly discuss.

Tragedy had by 415 moved away from the trilogy form of which Aeschylus' *Oresteia* is the outstanding example, and it is only rarely that we can detect connections among the groups of plays that later dramatists submitted to the festival. But *Trojan Women* comes at the end of what is almost certainly a 'Trojan trilogy', comprising the plays *Alexander* (another name for Paris), *Palamedes* (the name of a Greek warrior) and finally *Trojan Women*. While reconstruction of these plays is difficult, scholars concur on the broad lines.[45] The first play, *Alexander*, opened with Kassandra prophesying the downfall of Troy at the hands of Paris and recalling how she prophesied the same outcome when Hekabe was pregnant with Paris. Hekabe dreamed she gave birth to a flaming torch that set fire to the entire world, and was told by the Delphic oracles to put the baby to death. Since the baby was not put to death, but exposed, he was – inevitably – rescued and raised to manhood. During the course of the play the baby, now grown, comes to Troy to take part in athletic contests and, outrageously, wins, defeating the sons of the royal house. Hekabe moves from lamenting her lost child to plotting the murder of the upstart commoner, which is obviated when his identity is made known.

The second play, *Palamedes*, moves us straight from the early years of Paris to the height of the Trojan War. Set in the Greek camp, it concerns internal strife rather than hostilities against Trojans. Palamedes is the inventor of numerous benefits to the human community, such as writing, but Odysseus bears a grudge against him and concocts false accusations that get him executed by his own side. Since the final play is *Trojan Women*, set at the very end of the war, no play of this unusual 'trilogy' deals with the war itself on the territory staked out by the Homeric epic poems, and to that extent it may be considered slightly off-kilter and decentred. Critics have commented that the trilogy as a whole also sheds a different kind of light on *Trojan Women*. Although there are only rarely specific correspondences among the three plays (two of which of course are only reconstructions from fragments), there is at least one recurrent theme, the death of the innocent, and within this theme the thwarted death of Paris can render the death of Astyanax more comprehensible, because it is undertaken to avoid further disaster. Overall too, the high-octane atmosphere of the first two plays makes it more appropriate, in terms of pacing, that *Trojan Women* should eschew pretty much anything that counts as action.[46]

Pursuing the issues both of formal innovation and of relation to its trilogy, we might note that the opening of this play is remarkably like the ending of many others. Dunn points out that the way in which the gods appear and make dispositions for the future, which only come to fruition after the end of the dramatic action, is exactly what one might expect from the ending of a Euripidean play.[47] Overall, he suggests that the play 'starts at the end' and cannot move forward from there; a plot without plot development, it is a play of enforced inaction for both the women and the dramatist. *Trojan Women* does not seem to work through the consequences of the previous dramas as do other surviving 'third' plays like Aeschylus' *Eumenides* or *Seven Against Thebes*.

Melos in 416

While it is clear that *Trojan Women* is formally experimental, many readers have asked whether the play is not also discursively innovative in that it does draw directly on contemporary events, using the setting in Troy as a thin and penetrable disguise for a discourse about Athens. In the year before the production of the play, democracy and drama came together in surprising ways, and an event took place which passed into history in a way not available to other events. The island of Melos was a colony of Sparta's, but had managed for the course of the war to maintain sufficient neutrality to keep out of the way of both antagonists. In 416 this changed; Athens insisted that as an island, Melos should come over to her and should become a democracy.[48] The Melians refused, a siege ensued, the Melians were forced into unconditional surrender; the adult males were executed and the women and children sold as slaves.

The events at Melos are represented in Thucydides' *History* in highly memorable fashion. The 'Melian Dialogue' (5.17) purports to be a dialogue between Athenian ambassadors and oligarchic Melian leaders, before the Athenians begin to ravage the land, and it marks the only point in the *History* where the narrative voice falls silent, and the two parties to the dialogue speak one after another, direct discourse following the identifying name just as in a play script. While this is remarkable enough, still more striking is the content of what they say. Despite Thucydides' description of his practice in recording speeches outlined in Book 1, it is hard to maintain that this dialogue corresponds to his avowed principles, which are as follows (1.22):

> As for what each person said, either before the war or already in it, it was difficult for me to remember the exact wording either of the speeches that I heard myself or of those reported to me from elsewhere. I have made the speaker say what it seemed to me each would have found necessary to say in the various circumstances, keeping as close as possible to the overall idea of what was really said.

Few now believe Athenians or Melians said the words reported, let alone that they would have been what was necessary in the circumstances.[49] Not realism nor naturalism but high tragic discourse is what the Dialogue offers: the Athenians are clear-sighted and even comfortable in their ruthlessness; the Melians undeluded and fully conscious of their impossible position. Both speak at a high level of abstraction and generalisation, alike invoking the deities, the nature of imperial power, and the fortunes of war. Appealing to what is known or imagined of gods, the Melians remind the Athenians of the instability of human power or success, and also point to the calculations of honour and advantage that they must make. They do not omit to threaten the Athenians with the Spartans, who, as it happened, never came. In short, they speak from the heart of a traditional morality which may well no longer suffice for the situation they find themselves in; they are caught in the gap between the word and the world that has been opened up by the war, in which words have to change their meanings in accordance with new political exigencies, as dissected by Thucydides 3.82-3.[50] The Athenians, on the other hand, appeal quite straightforwardly to the power dynamics of the situation, and to the tendency of power to consolidate itself, which they note as a characteristic of the divine as much as of the human. Since their discourse explicitly repudiates any moral considerations in favour of the realities of unequal power, it can represent itself as alone equal to the situation and not liable to fall into the semantic gap between word and world. Stark alternatives, massive imbalance of power, traditional moral platitudes and radical revision of traditional morality alike squeezed out under pressure of extreme conflict; the Thucydidean narrative has chosen to recast whatever was said at Melos in terms of the period's most compelling art form, tragedy.

Did the suffering at Melos contribute even more directly to tragic discourse? Many readers have followed the lead of Gilbert Murray in seeing *Trojan Women* as a direct reference to Melos.[51] The men of Troy are dead and the women are slaves – and the Greeks who have orchestrated this will be punished, as we are told in the prologue, shipwrecked by a huge storm sent by Poseidon and Athena, and in addition, if we are to concur with such readers, consigned to the opprobrium of centuries. If translated to Athens in 416/15, Troy becomes Melos and Greeks become Athenians, excoriated for their deed of extermination and threatened with their own terrible reverses later on in the war. Since historically a city has recently been emptied, namely Melos, the argument holds that *Trojan Women's* focus on the destruction of a city must be readily understood to map Melos on to Troy; the devastation will in turn, the play warns, be visited on Athens. The argument acquires plausibility from the fact that tragedy regularly used the Trojan War to think through the Peloponnesian War.[52] Although rarely superimposing the one directly on to the other, it is unlikely that the plays of the late fifth century, such as Euripides' *Hekabe* and *Iphigeneia at Aulis*, did not take the Peloponnesian as well as the Trojan war into their purview when considering the significance and cost of war, and its effects on civil society.

The 'Melos interpretation' of *Trojan Women* is further assisted by the fact that Athens did indeed suffer disaster in the Sicilian campaign, which got underway in 415, and which could therefore be read as retribution for Melos. That Euripides could not have known what would happen at the end of the campaign, in 412, is not seen as an obstacle to this suggestion, because there may well have been doubt about how the war was proceeding, long before the end became obvious. We know, indeed, that doubt did exist about the Sicilian campaign at least, to the extent that the general Nikias warned the assembly against undertaking it (Thucydides 6.18). Doubt may even have extended to the conduct on Melos; as we have seen, the Athenians reversed their decision about comparable retribution at Mytilene, and this may have been from considerations of humanity as much as from the promptings of realpolitik detailed by Diodotos. While our sources cannot impose a decision on us, the notion that *Trojan Women* responds directly to Melos, and responds in a way that is presciently critical of Athens, has been found very compelling by many readers. The issue of identification is critical here too; if *Trojan Women* does indeed concern

Melos directly, then in order to interpret it properly the Athenians should have recognised themselves in the suffering Trojans *and* in the brutal Greeks.

There are also, however, several objections to this account of the play. The Melos interpretation relies on a fairly straightforward notion of representation where one city is coded for another, but there are arguments that militate against this understanding. For instance, Melos was not consigned to the flames and destroyed, because it was historically colonised by Athenians, and even inhabited again by Melian survivors who were settled there by the Spartans after 404 (Plutarch *Lysander* 14). Contrast this with the fate of Plataea in 427, razed by the Thebans (Thucydides 3.68), and not rebuilt until 382 (Pausanias 9.1-4).[53] On Melos the Athenians did not, as far as we know, sacrifice daughters of the island to shades of Athenian warriors or execute the children of prominent Melians; they kept to a level of atrocity which, some have argued, was simply too common during the Peloponnesian War to warrant wholesale condemnation, or even dramatisation.[54] Nor are the Athenians, as Athenians, notably castigated in *Trojan Women*. Although the sons of Theseus are keen for Polyxena to be sacrificed to Achilles, it is Odysseus who is most responsible for the death of Astyanax, and Athens is lauded in choral song as a desirable place to be (208-9). Other considerations have been assembled by other scholars, both practical and aesthetic. Erp Taalman Kip argues in detail from chronology that the play is too close to the massacre to be able to offer a critical commentary on it. Sidwell makes the different point that the play could express pity for the victims while not necessarily condemning the victors: 'Unlike ourselves, however, the Athenians could make distinctions between the pity to be accorded the victims of enslavement and the iron law of power politics which justified their enslavement.'[55] This dictum could hold for Melos as well as for Troy, and indeed in the case of Troy, the *Iliad* had habituated Greek culture to representing at one and the same time the noble heroes who sold their lives dearly for Troy and the misguided enthusiasts whose stubbornness ensured the downfall of their city. To represent the terror and pity of the fall is thus not necessarily to reproach the victors for it.

If we further recall that *Trojan Women* is the last play in a kind of trilogy, we might hesitate before subscribing completely to the Melos interpretation. Would there have been so easy a translation between the situations of Troy and Melos once Troy's fall became the culmination of a particular kind of story-telling rather than the isolated representation of wartime cruelties? It is perhaps hard to imagine a context in which Melos inspires a play, but requires that two more roughly connected plays be composed in order to go in front of it. Perhaps it is not necessary to imagine Melos as a specific inspiration, but rather as an additional consideration for a play which was already taking, overall, a sceptical approach to warfare. In other words, if we cannot say with any certainty that *Trojan Women* is anti-Melos, or anti-Athenian, can we say that it is anti-war? It has been hailed as a 'pacifist' play – 'the greatest piece of anti-war literature there is in the world'[56] – and its repeated staging in the twentieth century has plausibly been attributed to its ability to speak an anti-war message.[57] Whether or not such a stance was available in fifth-century Greece is highly debatable. The current scholarly consensus is that a peace movement recognisable in twentieth-century and later terms would not have been a possibility in ancient Greece; ancient Greek cities viewed peace as the hiatus between bouts of war rather than as the end to war.[58] Even those plays of Aristophanes which are generally accounted 'peace' plays, like *Acharnians*, *Peace* or *Lysistrata*, are not necessarily to be understood as opposing all wars, but as pleas for the end of a particular conflict. We might also note that some fifth-century sources, like the plays of Aristophanes, show the city population supporting the Peloponnesian War, while the country dwellers oppose it, so that calling for an end to the war might also be an intervention in internal Athenian politics. Nobody in *Trojan Women* expresses sentiments that are straightforwardly pacifist in a twentieth-century sense;[59] they lament their own sufferings, of course, but since Kassandra is happy to dream of revenge against Agamemnon and the Greeks, and Hekabe is happy to dream of what would have been Astyanax's future as overlord of Asia, it is not clear that anyone eschews the kinds of attitude that lead to warfare. Even Poseidon castigates not so much war itself as the sacking of cities, temples and graves (95-6). Kassandra's utterance at 400 comes close to a 'pacifist' statement in that she urges the man of sense always to shun war; but she goes on to acknowledge that it is sometimes necessary and that when it is, it is an adornment (literally *stephanos*, a garland) to a city to die a noble death (402).

The 'Melos interpretation' of *Trojan Women* is thus compelling but questionable. The Melos interpretation interrogates the Athenians' relations to their empire and their drama, but to consider it properly we must also examine our own assumptions. Do we respond enthusiastically to the notion of Euripides berating his countrymen chiefly because we are invested in a post-Romantic notion of the artist as isolated from and critical of his society? Such a notion of the artist may be inappropriate for the highly embedded dramatists of fifth-century Athens, whose plays formed the centrepiece of a civic festival with international dimensions. But at the same time, if we remove Melos from the play, we may stand convicted of a disregard akin to that of the Athenians in their imperial ruthlessness. We may perhaps not be convinced that the historical Euripides was deliberately using the stage to condemn the Athenians or induce them to run their empire differently. But it is hard to imagine that *Trojan Women* was not produced as part of a response to the historical Peloponnesian War and the toll it exacted in terms of political discourse as well as of lives and livelihoods. Neil Croally concludes that:[60]

> we are in no position to deny the possibilities of a contemporary audience finding – in many different ways, no doubt – references to the war they were engaged in as they watched the play ... This allowance must be made for all tragedy, but at the same time it should not be forgotten that the possibility of contemporary allusion is that much

more obvious in *Troades* than in some other plays (hence the academic debate about it).

This is a judicious assessment of a complex situation.

The play thus offers us two mutually exclusive interpretations – is it about Melos or not? – which also relate to internal divisions in the polis of Athens. This is a debate similar to that over how to understand the play as a whole, which has often polarised responses. At the extremes of interpretation are Murray, who invests in a version of *Trojan Women* as drawing beauty out of pain, music out of horror, and Adrian Poole, who reads nihilism without redemption.[61] Inasmuch as characters within the play, especially Hekabe, struggle to interpret their lives, each critical view is also supported by different moments in the play. As several critics note, Hekabe veers among different accounts of her life and cannot come to a final adjustment between despair that abandons effort and the attempt to wrench hope out of the situation.[62] The question of what sense to make of her predicament is handed over to the audience.

The audience are also invited, as I have suggested, to identify with those who are, in the ancient Greek context, as unlike them as possible, being a group of barbarian women captives. Even when the audience is not in fact composed of ancient Greeks, the gap between an audience viewing in relative security and comfort, and the plight of the women witnessing the end of their culture, is perhaps wider than some others posited by tragic dramas. This play then poses in extreme form the question that all tragedy invites us to, a version of which provides this book's epigraph. How does tragedy work with the relation between self and other – between 'Hecuba' and 'him'? The relations between self and other are, according to one argument at least, what give rise to the tragic responses of pity and fear. Identified as key components of tragedy by Aristotle, pity and fear are not fully defined in his canonical formulation in the *Poetics* (1449b), but possible definitions are illuminated by his account in the *Rhetoric* of pity and fear as dependent on the shifting positions of self and other. 'All things are to be feared which when they happen, or are on the point of happening, to others, excite compassion' (2.5); 'All that men fear in regard to themselves excites their pity when others are the victim (2.8)'.[63] The self and the other can occupy different positions on the spectrum of emotions, and crucially, they can identify with one another or even exchange places.[64] Since pity and fear are the emotions appropriate to tragedy (*Poetics* 1452b), to negotiate these varying relationships is the task presented to the audience, and this task may be intensified when we are told, as we are by *Trojan Women*, that victory and defeat, the results of which normally make it very clear which is self and which is other, are interchangeable. It is perhaps this structural variation, coupled with the extreme pitifulness of the play's representations, which has ensured that the play can speak significantly to many different contexts and conflicts. The pitiful representations concentrate on women and children, but the dialectic of self and other asks that adult males, the decision makers, imagine themselves equally vulnerable, and perhaps end by castigating themselves as equally culpable as the monstrous Greeks. In the twentieth century large-scale conflicts began explicitly to acknowledge civilians, women and children, as legitimate targets, which was the realisation that sent Gilbert Murray to the play in order to indict the British concentration camps during the Boer War, and which has helped to ensure the play's subsequent repeated appearances on stages throughout the world. The play's focus on women and children as victims, and its interrogation of the audience's relation to them, makes it more 'relevant' than is strictly desirable.

2

The Play

The gods

The play opens, as many Euripidean dramas do, with a deity, in this case Poseidon. Like many other prologue deities, he discharges a 'directorial' function,[1] explaining the current situation and announcing the future; we are in Troy, in the aftermath of its defeat, and the gods are leaving a city which can no longer honour them (23-7).[2] This city is depopulated to the extent that its only inhabitants are women and children, and the women are shortly not to be 'Trojan' at all; some have already been allotted to the different rulers of Greece and others, who are just off stage in tents, are prizes about to be divided up. As 'director', Poseidon introduces the main characters, mentioning Helen, Hekabe, Polyxena and Kassandra, and in fact directing the audience's attention to Hekabe with the words (36-7) 'This unhappy woman, if anyone wishes to look upon her, this is Hekabe, lying before the gates ...'.

Where this scene differs from other Euripidean prologues is that a second deity, Athena, suddenly enters the stage. While it is most common for a play to open without any deity, those tragedies which do have a divine prologue rarely have more than one god onstage; this is the case for *Ajax, Hippolytos, Bacchae* and *Ion.* Where there are two non-human beings, in *Alkestis*, only one of them is an Olympian, and the other is Thanatos, Death. Other prologues are delivered by non-human beings such as the ghost of Polydorus in *Hekabe*, where again there is only one figure on stage. In *Trojan Women*, Athena approaches Poseidon with a plan to disrupt the Greeks' homecoming. Although she has supported the Greeks throughout the

36

Trojan war, they have offended her by not punishing Ajax when he dragged the priestess Kassandra away from Athena's shrine, and they will accordingly be shipwrecked on the way home.[3] Athena comes to Poseidon to ask his help in sending a storm, but since Poseidon has been a supporter of Troy, she has her work cut out for her. What is strange about the encounter is that in the generally accepted mythical tradition Poseidon was an enemy to Troy because Laomedon, an earlier Trojan king, had cheated him and Apollo out of their pay when they built the walls of the city (*Iliad* 21.441). The god has thus done a volte-face, to which the play draws no attention, and Athena follows suit when she turns from supporting the Greeks to trying to destroy them. Such terrifying capriciousness, the logical consequence of untrammelled power, is characteristic of Euripidean gods, but perhaps nowhere else so strikingly dramatised.

The gods in the prologue thus determine that the Greeks' downfall will follow that of the Trojans, but the final significance of this divine caprice is left in doubt. Many readers argue that knowledge of the imminent destruction of the Greek fleet persists throughout the audience's witnessing of the destruction of Troy, providing, if not some moral balance, then at least some symbolic redress. While this is a consolatory interpretation which relates to Murray's notion that *Trojan Women* makes music out of a wrong, other readers stress that the Greeks are punished for one specific crime only, the outrage to Athena's shrine, and not for the blood shed in defeating and levelling Troy. [4] We might note in connection that Poseidon's parting speech does not condemn all war, but only the acts of sacking temples and graves. If we accept the restricted sense of this parting shot, it adds no weight to the argument that the play is in any sense anti-war, and the shipwreck does not console the Trojans, because it does not repay their sufferings, only the insult to the deity. Even if we do accept the notion of the shipwreck as some kind of redress for the Trojans' suffering, there are details in the play which seem to withdraw that hope. Kassandra gloats over the details of Agamemnon's death (353-64, 446-50), and Neoptolemos must hasten home because his grandfather is under attack (1123-30); and so far, the Greeks may be thought to experience condign punishment for the deaths they have caused. But when Kassandra details Odysseus' sufferings, and when, after the scene with Menelaos and Helen, the chorus pray that they may meet with shipwreck, these references to homecomings that might have been aborted only reinforce the realisation that in the mythical tradition these are quite successful. Possibly the most important thing we know about Odysseus is that he ends up safe and happy in Penelope's arms at home, after his tribulations; similarly, despite the storm described here and in Aeschylus' *Agamemnon*, we know from *Odyssey* 4 that Menelaos does not die at sea at all, but ends up in Helen's arms at home, even if not quite safe and not quite happy. Numerous disastrous Greek homecomings, known to us from other sources, are deliberately not invoked.

To call the play the tragedy of the Greeks, as much as of the Trojans, as do some critics,[5] seems then to betray the dreadful clear-sightedness of the play, by imagining a comforting justice where there is only the vast inequality of power obtaining between human and divine. The play proceeds partly as a demonstration of the corrosive effects of the inequality that obtains between conquerors and defeated, and it ends without a clear reminder of the reverses awaiting the power of the Greeks. Only by imaginatively projecting beyond the confines of the play itself can we assure ourselves of the desired just outcome, but it is not clear that we are encouraged to do so. On one persuasive reading, the 'beyond the play' is exactly what is missing from the end; although the play opens with a surfeit of deity, no god from the machine appears to close the play down with the reassurance that the human activity can and must be understood within some larger framework. Despite the liberal Euripidean use of the *deus ex machina*, often in situations where its presence is hardly welcome, there is here no divine reiteration of the Greeks' forthcoming dispersal. In turn, one of the most striking things about the unique beginning to *Trojan Women* is perhaps that it is matched by no comparable ending.

Instead, as we have noted, its beginning is a version of an ending, complete with valedictory address by a god, and between the two is only an endgame.[6]

Despite the clear-sightedness that I have invoked, however, to abandon the quest for justice or a moral settlement does not seem an adequate response, since justice persists in making elusive appearances throughout the play. For instance, Poseidon informs us that Helen is among the Trojan women, justly – *endikôs* – classed as a prisoner (35). The fact that she could be classed otherwise is, of course, what makes Poseidon's utterance here both necessary and questionable. The solemn pronouncement of Poseidon as the scene ends, declaring that those who sack cities and spoil temples and graves will themselves find destruction, might be seen to explain the shipwreck of the Greeks, but since it cannot account for the downfall of the Trojans, it still leaves open the question of justice. If we pursue the issue of what the Trojans might have done to bring the gods down on their heads, before the gods shifted their attention to the Greeks, we shall shortly end up like Helen in the scene of her debate with Hekabe, constructing ever more complex systems of blame. As we shall see at various different points in the analysis, however, blame, like justice, is extremely complex in this play, and an initial position of unequivocal sympathy for the Trojans may well be undermined in the course of the drama.[7]

Several readers go further and are ready to indict the Trojans. Anne Pippin Burnett argues that Troy is justly punished; culpable for her double dealings with the gods over the matter of the walls, and for her neglect of the honours done her by the gods' erotic entanglements, she suffers in correct proportion and the Greeks are merely the instrument of vengeance. This position has a sustained difficulty which certainly resonates with the moral contortions of Euripidean drama, and is attractive for this if for no other reason. It is harder to credit when we realise that it requires us to think the gods just and good at all times, a position to which we are not encouraged by this play or any other. But Burnett's analysis points to the important conclusion that Trojans may indeed be culpable along with Greeks; the past of Troy is at least as present to the play as is the future of Greece.

Christiane Sourvinou-Inwood has developed a similar analysis on different grounds, deriving from her argument that tragedy is part of the city's religious discourse. She places a good deal of emphasis on the agreement of the gods to destroy the Greeks, and especially on Poseidon's final pronouncement on the sacking of temples, which she claims 'establishes cause and effect and validates the notion of an ordered universe'. Because there is order, the Trojans too must have been culpable of something, and that something was to ignore the warnings that Hekabe's baby should not be allowed to live: 'Having watched the *Alexandros*, they [the audience] would have perceived the disasters to have been, first, predictable and predicted, and second, ultimately brought about by the fact that, when it came to it, the Trojan royal family ... had ignored the prophecies of the disaster'. It is thus at least arguable that the Trojans have contributed to their own sufferings. Following on from this, it is necessary that the audience should recognise that the gods do care about mortal affairs, and do uphold a principle of reciprocity; they have seen the gods caring about what mortals do in the prologue, and they have seen reciprocity at work even if only in a negative way. Sourvinou-Inwood can thus sum up: 'The Greek collective representations acknowledged that the world is cruel and precarious; the important thing is that there should be order and, in the main lines, justice guaranteed by the gods; and *Troades* says that there is.'[8] On this argument it is our inadequate notions of the divine, and not the gods themselves, which are challenged by the justice of the death of a child.

With the entrance of the deities there comes, as so often in Euripidean drama, an opaque discourse not only about gods but about human moral responsibility in the context of a universe largely unknowable, and often apparently hostile. The gods in *Trojan Women* divide critical opinion in the same way as does Melos. Even those interpretations of the divine that differ from

Pippin Burnett or Sourvinou-Inwood, however, commonly emphasise the fact that the audience sees the gods in action whereas the humans on stage never do. Thus Conacher suggests that the unfolding of the play leads Hekabe to the same point, in her apprehension of divinity, as the audience reaches immediately on witnessing the divine activities in the prologue.[9]

Poseidon's speech is programmatic in many other ways, even if on the question of justice it remains largely impenetrable. When he uses terms such as *erêmia* (emptiness, 15, 26), *phroudos* (gone, disappeared, 41), and *leipô* (to abandon, 25), he sets out a vocabulary of desolation that will be deployed repeatedly by the other characters.[10] He also puts into play the discourse of dancing and leaping, which will itself return in more deadly guises (755, 1206). Here, the dancers are the sea-nymphs who inhabit the depths of Poseidon's ocean (1-3), and it is Athena who leaps, in her shifting allegiances between Greek and Trojan (57). Much of the scene has an ironic cast, since while the two gods are united by family feeling (51), and the Greeks are happy to see again their wives and children (21), the Trojan women are completely bereft of all such connections. Connection is offered only by the Trojan landmarks, now full of the wailing of captive women (28); recalling a Homeric geography, the lines empty it of heroic content. One geographical marker is not so Homeric; Caphareus (90), listed as one of the places where the storm will strike, comes not from Homer but, arguably, from the second play in the Trojan trilogy. When Odysseus engineered the death of Palamedes, his father found out about his son's unjust execution and vowed vengeance on the Greeks; he promised to light deceptive beacons on the headlands at Caphareus which would lure the fleet on to the rocks as the Greeks journeyed homewards. Now that we know that the shipwreck will overtake the Greeks at Caphareus as well as elsewhere, the issue of justice and the Greeks' punishment becomes perhaps even more complex. Since the Greeks are to be shipwrecked by both human and divine intervention, we cannot tell whether the divine and human are invisibly cooperating in the Greeks' downfall or whether the one supersedes the other and the death of Palamedes, like other innocent deaths, is subsumed within the gods' calculations about their honour and prosecution of their revenge.

The gods are intimately involved with the history of Troy not only because Apollo and Poseidon helped to build its walls, but because gods have been the lovers of Trojans on numerous different occasions. As the chorus make clear in their various songs, the Trojan princes Ganymede (821), Tithonus (847-54) and Anchises, and the Trojan princess Kassandra, have all been recipients of divine erotic favours, usually to their own detriment. Recalling these associations, the chorus want to believe that they render the gods accountable to Troy, but are forced to conclude that such considerations do not always carry weight with the divine. Instead, the charms that captivated the gods have disappeared (*phrouda*, 858), and an entire verse of one song is dedicated to the proposition that Zeus has betrayed the sites of his own worship (1061-80). Andromache has come to the conclusion that the gods are destroying her (775-6), a characteristically tragic sentiment and one which is not necessarily vitiated by any inference that the gods will destroy the Greeks too. Hekabe alone has a more varied account of divinity, as befits her central place within the drama. She returns repeatedly to the paradox that the gods appear helpless or hostile, yet it is a persistent reflex to call on them (467, 1280); she rejects what she sees as their hostility towards Troy (612, 1240) yet continues to invoke them as witnesses to her plight (1288) and even, perhaps, gives them the credit for making Troy the subject of poetry to come (1242-5). At only one point in the play is there a noticeably different discourse about the divine, and that is during the *agôn* between Hekabe and Helen, to which we shall return.

The presence of the gods at the opening of the play, compounded by their absence at the ending, poses very acutely the questions of justice that the play declines, within the confines of its life on stage, to answer unequivocally. That the play is part of a trilogy which may have included elements pointing to some guilt on the part of the Trojans does not necessarily make the Trojan women's suffering easier, for them or for us.

2. The Play

Hekabe

Visible on stage for the length of the play, even when fallen in a huddled heap, the protagonist is in an almost unparalleled theatrical situation. Her role is to engage with the other named characters in sequence, and over and above this, it is Hekabe, with the chorus, who gives emotional expression to the fall of Troy. With the chorus she shares lyric passages, especially towards the beginning and at the end of the play; she engages in antiphonal laments with Andromache and also gives a series of substantial speeches, or *rhêseis*. These vary in their nature depending on her interlocutor. With Kassandra she does little except remonstrate with her apparently deranged daughter, but when Kassandra leaves, Hekabe speaks at length about her own plight (466-510); with Andromache, she makes a speech designed to encourage and fortify her daughter-in-law (686-708), but falls silent after the announcement by Talthybios of Astyanax's death. In the scene of the *agôn* with Helen her speech is of a quite different nature, over 60 lines long (969-1032), but she returns to the role of *mater dolorosa* with the lament over the body of her grandson (1156-1206).

Hekabe punctuates the action in other ways too, notably with her body. Lying on the ground during the gods' prologue, she then raises herself, only to fall again after the emotionally exhausting scene with Kassandra (462-8). She is perhaps on the ground again, though not prostrate, when the shield of Hektor, bearing the body of Astyanax, is brought in and placed on the ground (1156), and Hekabe addresses the boy's different features and the shield's different parts. It is hard to conclude that she does not touch them as she speaks, and to touch them she must presumably be on their level. Finally, at 1305, Hekabe sinks to the ground and with her the chorus women, to beat the earth of Troy and call upon the dead whom they are leaving. She must therefore rise in order to leave the stage on her way to Greece.

As well as bearing the brunt of the play physically, Hekabe occupies the centre discursively. Inasmuch as she repeatedly endeavours to make sense of the overwhelming events around her, she is a very self-conscious speaker, reflecting on the nature of her interventions even as she makes them (e.g. 120-1, 1148-52). Readers have commented that the rhythm of the play is the rhythm of Hekabe's responses to the various crises she encounters, likening this mostly to a rise and fall as she seems to give up but then retrieves resources with which to go on.[11] Where we judge that she ends up, on the rise or on the fall, is related to whether we judge the play to be ultimately nihilistic or to salvage something from the ruins. Perhaps it makes little sense for us to judge at all; we might instead acknowledge that the play simply *is* the series of struggles endured by Hekabe and the chorus women, with no access to a larger story. That there is no *deus ex machina* perhaps indicates the difficulty of finding a scheme within which to deliver a final understanding of the play.

The characteristic features of Hekabe's speeches in the drama are the following: a discourse on the gods, which we have already noted; a discourse on the history of Troy, not unlike that given by the chorus, but which dwells more on Troy's wealth and glamour; a discourse on music, singing and dancing, and its consolatory effects; a discourse about ships and the sea which perhaps relates to her destiny as a Greek slave;[12] a pervasive self-consciousness about her acts and her speech which perhaps is a sign of her regal calling. In her first appearance she likens her fortunes to a ship at sea (102-4) and later on addresses the very ships which brought Helen and so can be seen to have started all her troubles (122-31). She addresses the various parts of her aged, aching body (112-18) and describes her mourning itself (106-7, 110-11): 'What is not here for me to mourn in my misery, whose country has gone and children and husband? ... What must I silence? What not silence? What must I mourn?' Crucially, she remarks on the paradox whereby song about misery itself is a consolation in the midst of misery: 'music itself to the unhappy [is] to sing of ruin that does not let us dance' (120-2).[13] She closes the speech with an injunction to the chorus women to lament with her, as if they were singing with her in the old days, and she specifically compares this choral activity with the dances she led at Troy (146-52), thus presenting the first of the play's contrasts to Poseidon's dancing Nereids.

In two respects Hekabe retains a significant notion of herself as queen of Troy. She frequently invokes its previous wealth, beginning here with 108-9 where she laments the wealth that has disappeared. Secondly, on occasion she sees herself as responsible for the other women, calling herself a mother bird at 146, and at 159 and 182, calling them children.[14] This attitude does not often surface amid the lamentations for her own fallen state; what she does do for the women, however, is to address them in very Homeric terms, repeatedly recalling the epic grandeur of Troy. Thus at 143 the chorus women are wives of the bronze-speared Trojans, even though there are no Trojans left. The sea is purple (124) and the chorus women themselves call their lodging 'halls' rather than tents (154). Kassandra will do something similar when she addresses the chorus women, ironically, as 'beautifully robed' (*kallipeploi*, 338).

The chorus

The Trojan chorus women represent themselves mostly as wives with children, although elements of their songs are appropriate for young and perhaps even unmarried women. With Hekabe they share the task of lamentation, and with Andromache the horror of being forced to the conqueror's bed; at 684 Andromache's description of her plight teaches them to know their own. Although there are thus bonds among the captured women, the chorus are aware that they are not the principal characters in this play, and they memorably remark at 293-4 that while Hekabe knows her fate, theirs is still obscure. Like Hekabe, however, they have a rhetorical sense of their own songs, prefacing their song about the Horse with the note that it is a new kind of hymn, one accompanied by tears (512-14) and remarking on the sweetness, to the unhappy, of tears, dirges and laments, and sad music (608-9).

The chorus sing at crises in the action, beginning with their first song when they enter, fearfully, from the Greek tents, in the disorder of two half choruses that have yet to unite. There are no songs where the singers long to flee from the dramatic situation, such as are often thought to exemplify Euripidean escapism; rehearsing the history of Troy in order to try to make sense of its hurtful present and its lack of future, the songs are closely tied to the action. The first song is different, because it concentrates on Greece, but it begins with the chorus women lamenting the loss of the loom that they will never use and the parents whom they will never see again. They then move to thoughts of the land where they are bound, and commentators have remarked that the play as a whole is signally oriented towards the future, even as it devotes energies to recalling the past.[15] Here, the chorus women represent their Greek destination in surprisingly favourable terms, describing the fertility and beauty of several Greek locations, including, prominently, Athens (207-8, 214-29). The only spot that is anathema is Sparta, home of Menelaos and Helen.

One element of the song here has other particular resonances in the rest of the play. The chorus mention the garland or *stephanos* (223) which will reappear several times, usually as a sign of victory or celebration, but on occasion with darker connotations, as when Astyanax is taken to the 'coronet' (*stephanos*, 785) of the city walls. To trace how the *stephanos* migrates among the characters gives a sense of the complexities of the play's discourse on victory and defeat.[16]

The chorus' other songs, which we shall look at in further detail in their places, describe a kind of arc of remembrance, moving away from the present moment and then returning to it. Each comes at a point in the action at which Hekabe has fallen silent under the weight of misfortune. The second song takes over after Hekabe, in despair at the departure of Kassandra, longs to cast herself down and perish in the ravages of tears (507-8); the third when, overcome by the parting from Astyanax, she wonders what is missing from their wholesale destruction (797-8). The fourth song comes as Helen leaves for safety and success in Greece. Together these songs attempt to construct a history of Troy, although it is not always one that makes sense. Treating the night when the Wooden Horse was brought into Troy, the second song (511-76) dwells on the ghastly contrast between the joy of its reception and the agony of Troy's end; the third (799-858) gives a different version of Troy's history that moves between its multiple defeats at the hands of heroes – Herakles in the past, the Greeks in the present – and the divine desire that has repeatedly picked out Trojan males for its object. The two sides of this history cannot be coordinated except to realise, as noted above, that the love charms are now lost (*phrouda*, 858). This realisation works through the fourth song, which as we have seen accuses the gods more explicitly of betrayal, listing the natural features of Troy, and its religious rites, that the gods have deserted. In its description of lost husbands and abandoned children, this song emerges at the present, again imagining parts of Greece where the women may end up, and where they hope Menelaos and Helen never will. This is the last full song in the play; the ending is made up of lyric exchanges between Hekabe and the chorus, mourning for Astyanax and for Troy as they depart.

Talthybios

Hekabe and the chorus persist throughout the drama; each of the three Trojan princesses, conversely, dominates her scene and then leaves. Only one character punctuates the action with a number of separate appearances, and that is the herald Talthybios. Apart from Menelaos in his scene, it is Talthybios who orchestrates what happens, bringing in the news of the Greeks' dispositions and taking the women away, and much of the play therefore consists of the women's reactions to his announcements. Inasmuch as he is almost the only male and almost the only Greek that we see on stage, it is telling that he is not a male or a Greek in power; he too is at the disposal of the Greek commanders, and admits on occasion to fear of them (304-5). We shall not be surprised to find that he polarises readers between those who find him human and sympathetic and those who find him a cold and even callous functionary.[17] Is he simply a mouthpiece of his Greek masters, or do we watch him increasingly baffled and tormented by the duties he must discharge? Since the messages he brings originate elsewhere, his initiative is confined to other sorts of actions; consequently we should not underestimate his spontaneous gesture, towards the end, of bathing the corpse of Astyanax and washing clean the wounds.

Despite his orchestration of events, the Trojan women often ignore him. When he first enters and addresses Hekabe, with a familiarity that he explains by their repeated encounters during the war (235-8), she does not immediately respond to him but turns to the chorus women instead. Similarly, after he has spoken to Kassandra and Hekabe, Kassandra speaks of him in the third person and does not deign to address him directly for a couple of lines (424-6). When he announces the decision about the death of Astyanax, Andromache must engage with him, but when he leaves the scene expressing his reluctance to carry out his orders, nobody on stage responds (786-9). At 1156 Hekabe acknowledges nothing of Talthybios' speech about washing the body, and when Talthybios makes his final appearance, to direct the burning of Troy, he no longer speaks to the Trojan women, but only to the Greek captains whose task it is to set the fires.

These gulfs between Talthybios and his interlocutors arise partly, of course, because of the nature of the messages that he must deliver. In his first appearance he remarks that the women might try to kill themselves, because noble women could not stand to be slaves; although they do not ever do so, the lines suggest that Talthybios has the correct measure of their situation.[18] While he is quite obtuse about Kassandra's future, claiming that it is a great thing for her to go to the bed of a king (259), he has considerable difficulty articulating Polyxena's fate and in fact does not ever tell Hekabe explicitly that her daughter is dead. At the close of the scene with Kassandra he expresses his distaste for her discourse and person and distances himself from the king who, while being in charge of the Greeks, is deranged enough to desire this abrasive female (413-16). He distances himself still further from the Greeks when he brings in the decision to execute Astyanax; in three different ways he expresses his reluctance to utter the words and at the end of the scene, says that someone who feels no pity, and less shame, should do the job (710, 713, 717, 786-9). The contorted nature of the last phrases perhaps points again to the difficulty of what he is required to do.

Before he leaves with Astyanax, he makes a short speech to Andromache impressing on her how she should behave in this unprecedented situation. Talthybios requires Andromache to embrace her own powerlessness and not to provoke the Greeks in any point, in case she not be allowed to bury her son properly. Where readers differ is over whether he does this out of arrogance or a kind of misplaced kindness, with several critics on each side.[19] In performance, a decision about how he delivers this homily would be inescapable, whereas the other kinds of equivocation that we have examined would not necessarily be solved by theatrical choices.[20] What may be relevant is that the more we understand the herald and his boss Menelaos as ordinary and ineffectual, the more they become a version of 'us'. Like Athenians in 415, we are invited to see ourselves in the suffering Trojan victims but also in the predatory Greeks.[21]

Kassandra

Kassandra enters bearing the torch that frightened Talthybios, singing and dancing in celebration of her imminent 'wedding' to Agamemnon. She persists in so naming her forthcoming sexual submission, despite the pleas of Hekabe and the chorus, and only departs from her celebratory wedding songs in order to give a resounding speech about the 'victory' of the Trojans over the Greeks.[22] How she argues this is because the Trojans die gloriously defending their homes, tended by loved ones; the Greeks die far from home and are only there in the first place because of the shameful adultery of Helen and the abominable sacrifice of Iphigeneia (368-405). Reprimanded by Talthybios, she rounds on him with vivid description of the coming sufferings of Odysseus (431-43) and the death of Agamemnon (446-7). She tears Apollo's garlands from her head and rushes off to the ships still triumphant (451-61).

As David Raeburn writes, Kassandra's long and demanding scene constitutes a real 'number'.[23] Its energy and excitement are such that it is hard to see how the old charge of static immobility could have any force. Such a charge is much less prevalent in the current critical context where performance is important, but the scene is not merely visually spectacular, because it also constructs discursive relationships with other dramas. Kassandra brings with her the first play of Euripides' 'Trojan trilogy', in which she appeared, perhaps in the prologue, to announce the fall of Troy that is presaged by the survival of Hekabe's firebrand son, Alexander/Paris. It is probably she alone who was aware of the shepherd's true identity as he came to take on all comers in Troy. Unheeded then, her words now too will have little impact on her internal audience.

The Kassandra scene in Aeschylus' *Agamemnon* provides other parameters.[24] In that scene and this, Kassandra first speaks in a delirium and then more lucidly, foretelling the death of Agamemnon and herself, dreaming of revenge, and representing her extremity by tearing off the insignia of the god. In *Agamemnon*, Kassandra sees through the ghastly history of her new home; in *Trojan Women*, she similarly penetrates to a truth about the current situation that is at first elusive and always unpalatable. Although the mythical tradition claims that Kassandra can never be believed, the dramas deal differently with this affliction. The chorus in *Agamemnon* claim that they have no trouble believing her when she describes the history of the Atreid house, but they simply cannot understand her when she foretells the death of Agamemnon – they cannot grasp that the wife will murder the husband. In *Trojan Women*, as we shall see, Kassandra's on-stage interlocutors have varying reactions to her speech, but both Kassandra-figures are isolated on stage, even if communicating, perhaps obliquely, with the audience.

2. The Play

Kassandra's lyric monody on marriage here, which is how she represents her sexual slavery, is the first of a series of discussions of marriage that will punctuate the play.[25] The chorus have already brought up the possibility that they will go to the beds of Greeks in the parody of marriage that awaits concubines and female slaves; the three 'daughters' of Hekabe will each discuss marriage or a perversion of it; and even the death of Astyanax will be described in terms of the marriage he did not have. Given that marriage is not a matter of choice, for ancient Greek women, it eloquently illustrates the absence of freedom that characterises the lives of all women, not just Trojan slaves, and also provides a template for managing situations of restricted agency. As a ritual, moreover, marriage speaks to one of women's characteristic cultural contributions, and the women of Troy will continue to preserve the forms of civilisation by performing the impoverished versions of ritual that are all that is now left to them. Kassandra will thus organise her own 'wedding', orchestrating the roles for her mother and the chorus of mock bridesmaids (332-41), and Hekabe and the chorus will later on improvise a funeral for Astyanax.

Despite these considerations, the question remains: why does Kassandra describe her forthcoming sexual subjugation to Agamemnon in terms of a properly ordered and celebrated marriage, the sort that young girls conventionally welcome as well as fear? One answer is that she is mad, but the nature of her madness then invites investigation. As she is a priestess and prophetess of Apollo, we might assume that her madness is caused by the god's possession, and if so, her description of her future must be understood as inspired by the god. Alternative scenarios also leave room for Kassandra to be correct. We noted above that the rhythm of her scene corresponds to that of the Aeschylean Kassandra, with a delirium that subsides into 'normal' speech, but we might add that Phaidra in Euripides' *Hippolytos* follows the same pattern. Despite delirium, both the Aeschylean Kassandra and Phaidra speak the truth – Kassandra describes past and future accurately, while Phaidra gives voice to her desire for Hippolytos, even if in obscure and de-flected terms. Even if Kassandra in *Trojan Women* were not possessed by Apollo, we might conceive that she speaks the truth as Phaidra does, through her delirium. There is a kind of truth in her celebration of this 'wedding', because the bride will bring death to the commander of the Greeks. Kassandra's concubinage is, then, a source of pleasure and comfort to her, as a proper marriage would ideally be, and her mother and the other women of Troy would also be consoled if they could see into the future as she can.

Some critics contend that Kassandra has lost her mind under the pressure of the misery of Troy's fall, and that rape and enslavement have deprived her of her reason. She is deluded with 'the unclouded simplicity and happiness of one who in madness is oblivious to the real circumstances', or is in a state of frenzy.[26] But others conclude that Kassandra's madness is grounded in a perception of reality different but equally valid. Lee notes that she expresses 'the emotions of a woman who sees her fate as it really is'.[27] For Gregory, she is 'just as sound as she always was', and her madness is 'sardonic' and 'ironic',[28] while for Mossman Kassandra takes literally what the world sees as metaphors.[29] The ambiguity is perhaps summed up when Kassandra states, in her iambic passage of speech, as opposed to song, that although she is *entheos*, inspired or possessed, liter-ally with god in her, she will stand outside her bacchic transports in order to explain her position on defeat and victory (366-7). She is not, then, too mad to give up being mad.

For me the most compelling interpretation is that Kassandra is very much in control, clear-sighted, and ironic rather than mad. This is not to detract from the theatrical power of her mad scene – but it is to stress that the madness itself is theatrical, staged for a specific purpose. Kassandra delights in the irony of celebrating slavery and rape as marriage, but is protected from the horror of that equation by her knowledge not only of the future but of the real significance of the present. Kassandra celebrates her forthcoming 'wedding' because her union with Agamemnon is genuinely to be welcomed, signifying as it does his imminent and brutal demise at the hands of his other wife. Furthermore, in this way she takes control of the representation of her situation; we can see this in the contrast with the Aeschylean Kassandra who is trying to get people to recognise what is, rather than describing what is in different terms. There is almost humour in her injunction to her mother to hurry her along even though she may be reluctant – like a proper *parthenos* about to lose her virginity (355-6). She is well aware of what other people think of the reality of the situation, remarking on Hekabe's constant lamentation and comparing the present to the days when Priam reigned (315-18, 327).

Hekabe and the chorus greet the celebration with grief and dismay because they are not privy to Kassandra's knowledge of Agamemnon's death. To her outrageous statements about the nature of victory and defeat they make no response, and it is unlikely that they take her seriously. The response is left to Talthybios, who shows that he has understood completely what Kassandra means, and is highly offended by it, but can disregard it, like the chorus of *Agamemnon*, because he believes she is raving (408-10, 417-19). Her 'madness' then permits her to say what nobody else could, and get away with it. She continues to exploit this possibility when she is dismissive of Talthybios and his herald's function at 424-6. The price of this freedom is to be unable to communicate it.

The issue of belief in Kassandra's words is important for the audience in the theatre as well as for the internal audience on the stage. Kassandra argues not only that the day of her slavery and concubinage is to be celebrated because it is in fact the beginning of the end for the leader of the Greeks, but also that in any case, the Greeks are worse off after the fall of Troy. She does not invoke the coming shipwreck, although she does detail the tribulations waiting for Odysseus; she argues instead, as we have seen, that the Trojans gained the glory, and the Greeks go away with shame and dishonour (365-405). The significances of victory and defeat are inverted. She thus asks the women on stage, and us, to believe an impossible thing, an unmanageable paradox which will be, it turns out, only the first of several which will assault Hekabe, the chorus women, and the audience, in the course of the play.

Kassandra's inversion of victory and defeat has played a significant part in the 'Melos interpretation'; drawing on Kassandra's words, the argument holds that the apparent Athenian success in the Peloponnesian War, and especially on Melos, is hollow and deceptive, and that the Athenians are already in some sense the losers that they will shortly be seen to be on Sicily and at Aegospotami. We concluded earlier that it is hard to posit a one-to-one equivalence between the events on Melos and the representations in *Trojan Women*, but we may acknowledge that the overall account of inversion between victory and defeat is compelling in its perversity. For audiences in the late twentieth and early twenty-first centuries the inversion becomes more compelling as the era's conflicts throw up more equivocal outcomes. For those audiences too, the Melos interpretation gains support from the figure of Kassandra, who might be understood as a metaphor for a poet desirous of intervening in politics yet wary of audience displeasure; poet and prophetess alike tell truth to power obliquely, and get away with it.

We also have to wonder if we have understood Kassandra correctly. If she cannot be believed, why would we trust her bold inversion of victory and defeat? Have we perhaps completely misunderstood what she is saying? We might invoke here the formulation of Vernant and Vidal-Naquet, two of the seminal critics of the later twentieth century, who suggest that the 'tragic message, when understood, is precisely that there are zones of opacity and incommunicability in the words that men exchange'.[30] According to the analysis, these barriers to communication among characters on stage can be resolved at the level of the spectator. That the spectator is more empowered than the characters is indeed a possible conclusion, but it also assumes a separation between stage and spectator that may not be warranted. If all the spectators see is confusion on the part of the characters, how can they be sure that they are not also caught up in its dynamic? Kassandra's scene thus asks quite aggressively where the stage ends and the spectator begins; this is a question posed on a larger scale by the dramatic dynamic between self and other, and coordinated with the identities of victory and defeat.

Despite the compelling qualities of much of Kassandra's discourse, it is not completely consistent with itself, even in the iambic passages that are usually considered more 'sane' than the lyrics (368-405). While dismissing Agamemnon's choice to sacrifice Iphigeneia rather than quit the campaign, she none-theless repeats the tenets of the traditional heroic code when describing Hektor and Paris, claiming that their glorious deaths and heroic memories outweigh any mortal sufferings (394-9).[31] Indeed, as we have seen, she expressly praises the glorious death as a garland, *stephanos*, won for the city, even though a wise man will in general shun war (400-2). Although she questions the traditional categories of defeat and victory, she is utterly unequivocal about her victory over Agamemnon – it does count as victory, not defeat, and for it she is to be twice acclaimed with the epic term *nikêphoros*, bringer of victory (353, 460).

In the aftermath of Kassandra's monody, Hekabe and the chorus react differently. Hekabe falls to the ground and does not want to get up, but she retains discursive control and self-awareness. While she terms the gods poor allies, she concedes that somehow to call on them is unavoidable (469-70); it is also possible for the audience to perceive the gods at work in the foretold death of Agamemnon, which would indicate that Hek-abe is wrong in her assessment of them as allies. Hekabe's speech is in spoken iambics, not sung lyrics, but it recapitulates some of the topics of her first monody. Deliberately contrasting her present sufferings to the great happiness she enjoyed be-fore, she is aware that this discourse increases pity (473). She closes with a sentiment attributed to Solon: 'call no man happy until he is dead' (509-10). Usually characterised as quintessen-tially Greek, the sentiment may seem anomalous in the mouth of a Trojan. In this same speech, at 477, Hekabe boasts of children such as no Trojan, Greek or barbarian woman ever had. Although there are thus three categories, the Solonic apothegm may be considered to align the Trojan with the Greek, over against the barbarian. In the later stages of the play different speakers will indicate that the barbarian may be closely identified with the Trojan, or more disturbingly, with the Greek.

Following Hekabe's account of pity, the chorus begin their song with a self-conscious description of its tearful strangeness and novelty. Describing the epiphany of the Wooden Horse in Troy and the destruction that ensued, this song, like the 'mad' song of Kassandra and the more sober words of Hekabe, foregrounds singing and dancing, but here only to ironic effect. Dominant within the song is the figure of the young girl or virgin *parthenos* (527, 545, 536), entrusted with the task of singing and dancing for the community on important occasions like this of the welcome for the Horse. The chorus members are assimilated to these *parthenoi* (551-5), but they also sing of children clinging to their mothers' clothes (557-9). These children are implicitly contrasted with those engendered by the rapes (563-7), as the young girls become the young women (*neanidai*) who are impregnated by the side of their husbands' dead bodies and thus pass the crown of triumph (*stephanos*, 565) to Greece.

Andromache

Combining the figures of virgin girl and woman, the song bridges the gap between Kassandra and Andromache, and the mention of children opens the way for the entrance of Astyanax's mother, on a wagon, with her son clinging to her bosom (568-76). Heaped with the treasures of Troy and the weapons of Hector, the wagon will provide the son of Achilles with spoil to decorate the temples. The verb *stephô* (garland, 575) evokes the garland or *stephanos* which moves, as we have seen, between Trojan and Greek to indicate the transience of victory and defeat. Andromache's entrance is just as striking as the all-singing, all-dancing entrance of Kassandra, invoking as it does a number of other earlier dramatic chariot entrances such as those of Atossa in *Persians*, Agamemnon in *Agamemnon*, and Klytemnestra in Euripides' *Elektra*. Comparison with other such entrances indicates that they mark the point of a precipitous fall from prosperity to doom.

From 577 Andromache and Hekabe engage in a lyric exchange of lamentation, each taking part of a line. Even within the exclamations their utterances are knitted together syntactically, so that they are more connected in dialogue than was, say, Hekabe with Kassandra during her song. At 595 the metre changes for a few lines to dactylic hexameters, an epic metre, so that it more deliberately recalls Homeric poetry. It is at this point that Andromache introduces a sour note into their joint lament because she points to the role of Hekabe's son in the downfall of Troy (597).[32] This downfall is described in terms of a hateful bed (*lechos*), for the sake of which Paris destroyed a city, and a yoke of slavery (*zeugos*) which is now imposed on Troy. Both the bed and the yoke will reappear in Andromache's speech, speaking of the kinds of associations which are either made or broken in this moment of Troy's end (666, 670, 678). Beside these images is the description of the dead bodes that lie at the feet of Athena (599-600); while these are unburied and ready for the vultures, both Andromache and Hekabe will be involved in providing proper rites for the unburied dead.

From 608 the two women seem almost to vie in describing their immiseration. When Hekabe recounts the loss of Kassandra, Andromache replies with the news of Polyxena's death; she left the wagon to cover the body with a robe and to cut her hair in mourning, performing the kind of correct ritual actions that would help to repair the rents in the social fabric were it not already completely shredded. The death of Polyxena also serves to motivate the debate between Hekabe and Andromache, during which Andromache endeavours to convince her mother-in-law of the play's second paradox, namely that death is preferable to life in sorrow (636-7). Hekabe resists this conclusion, although she herself has said something not unrelated, 'the dead man forgets his pains' (606). Here instead she urges that life and death not be conflated, because the one is nothing, the other offers hope (632-3). Hope is embodied in Astyanax, who must be raised to help and even to settle Troy again (702-5). The news of Astyanax's impending death puts an end to this plan.

Before we are forced to confront the sentence on Astyanax, however, Andromache makes her long speech in praise of death. Polyxena's oblivion is preferable to the radical disjunction that Andromache is forced to live through between what was prescribed for her as wife of Hektor and what she must now endure. Her account of what 'life' is, as opposed to death, is an account of how she managed her marriage to Hektor, and relates to Kassandra's representation of her sexual slavery as marriage. Although Andromache has worked hard to be a successful wife, her success has won her only the opportunity, indeed the necessity, to abandon the memory of Hektor in the bed of a new master. She copes with this harsh paradox by refuge in the other paradox, the preference for death.

As well as being pertinent to the present situation, Andromache's description of herself as ideal wife invokes the version in *Iliad* 6. Some critics have found the rhetorical quality of *Trojan Women* occasionally forced and not related to character,[33] but we should note that character is not all that is at stake during a tragic performance; relationships to earlier poetry are also important in determining the significance of the tragic language and suggesting responses to it. We might also note that it would be hard for rhetoric to relate to character in *Trojan Women*, because the people in the play are improvising in unprecedented situations – they no longer have the characters that they used to have. Andromache's speech struggles to relate her past life to her future, which is the task that all the Trojan women face, and her language can bridge the gap no more easily than her lived experience can.[34]

In *Iliad* 6 Andromache is supremely articulate and clear-sighted. She deals with her husband Hektor on a basis of equality, advising him on how to win the war as well as on other topics, but she also knows what will happen to herself and her son in the event of Troy's defeat. In the play, her version of a successful marital partnership is not all about submission, for as Gregory points out, she asserts herself aristocratically,[35] and again, she has few illusions about the future. Like many of the other women speakers she is self-conscious about the status of her discourse and introduces it, paradoxically, as a 'most beautiful argument' which will cast pleasure into Hekabe's mind.[36]

Questioning the Greek commonplaces about the ungovernability of women, Andromache's speech is about her moral agency and self-control as a wife. She aimed at a reputation for *sôphrosunê*, which connotes various dispositions suitable for women such as chastity and reticence, and which is often translated 'prudence' in English. In pursuit of this reputation, Andromache trained herself not to want to go outside her house or to let the gossip of women inside it (650-2). Sufficient to herself (653), she presented a quiet tongue and tranquil eye to her husband, but still knew when each partner should 'win' in the relationship. The irony of her use of the 'victory' verb here (*nikan*, 655) is similar to the irony of her whole doomed attempt at virtue. The control that she fought for is lost, because Neoptolemos now desires this domestic paragon for his concubine. So how should she comport herself? Should she be a traitor to the memory of Hektor, or cling to the memory and be hated by her new master? The kind of sexual mobility that characterises the fall of the city threatens to make a mockery of Andromache's previous life by turning all women into Helen, and her self-control is further menaced by the proverbial wisdom she has heard, that one night suffices to reconcile a woman to a new man (665-6). While women are thus by definition not amenable to sexual self-control, Andromache instances animals who show fidelity to their lost partners (669-70). Forced even to know that she thus has no cause for hope, Andromache ends her demonstration with a return to Polyxena as an example of the oblivion she craves (679-83).

Andromache's meditation on women's self-control is related to the interventions by the other 'daughters' of Hekabe. Kassandra showed a woman apparently out of control, yet aware that she would have unmistakable effects on the future. Helen's discourse will stress how far beyond her control her circumstances are, yet the speech itself will ensure that she emerges triumphant. These meditations on human effectiveness in a universe apparently hostile were of as sharp a relevance to fifth-century Athens as would have been a drama that specifically envisaged the destruction of Melos and the Athenians' condign punishment.

Hekabe responds to Andromache's speech with a discourse of her own on the issue of control, which she eventually advises Andromache to relinquish. Although Hekabe has never been on a ship, she has seen pictures, and she understand that sailors in a storm govern the ship for as long as they can, but give up when the sea overwhelms them. So Andromache should forget Hektor and try to love Neoptolemos, if only in order to protect her son (686-705). The contradictions multiply in this short utterance, since seamanship was regularly invoked in the fifth century as a sign of human mastery, not of its limits, and also because the control that Hekabe seems to advise giving up returns, in the guise of protecting Astyanax. It is also very different from the advice that Hekabe later says she gave Helen, which was to cling to past affections rather than be swayed by present force. But to emphasise the contradictions may be to misconstrue the identity of the speech; perhaps it is not at all an account of what Hekabe actually thinks, but an attempt to make Andromache's situation more bearable – 'rhetoric' of a dismally necessary kind.[37] There *is* a gap between the word and the world, and the language that tries to bridge it also calls attention to the yawning chasm beneath the bridge.

Talthybios enters to ratchet up the agony of the Trojan women, and perhaps of the audience, still further, with the death sentence for Astyanax. No longer using the familiarity which he adopted with Hekabe, he addresses Andromache as 'former wife of the best of the Phrygians' (709), which is an epic, heroic address but also one that implicitly explains why the son of that father must die. The messenger cannot identify with his task as blithely as he did when distributing the women, but what managing there can be, Talthybios recommends to Andromache; she must realise her position, living up to her aristocratic status only insofar as she does not presume strength where there is none (727-8). The Greeks are well able to fight one woman, especially since – we might add – they have been fighting over one woman the whole time (731-2). 'Shameful' or 'provocative' action – other than the sentence itself – and curses called down on Greek heads, are proscribed, in the interests of assuring Astyanax a proper burial. Andromache's self-control is to be called to a last and most dreadful test. [38]

Andromache's farewell to her son is profoundly moving; having made one speech as wife she must now make another as mother, and she gathers together familiar tropes that do not lose their power through familiarity, such as the lost labour of the mother and the sweet smell of the child's flesh (757-60). These tropes she puts into new relations with accounts of the child's Trojan heritage, as when she calls him *perissa timêtheis*, excessively honoured (740), and speaks of his imagined future as a *tyrannos*, overlord, of Asia (748). While the mother is powerless to save the son, the father is even more culpable, because it is his nobility that causes the son's death (742-3). These lines are particularly intriguing because a note by scholiasts suggests that a version of them featured in the first play of the trilogy, where it concerned there the death of Paris. The two innocent children, Paris and Astyanax, are compared directly, in very early readings of the play if not in the authorial holograph.

Andromache's control slips for one moment, when she explodes at the Greeks (766) 'Oh you Greeks, who have invented barbarian evils'. The force of the outburst depends on the audience's recognising that the Greeks should not be barbarians, but that the Trojans are; the alignment here is different from in Hekabe's speech where there were three categories, Greek, barbarian and Trojan. But Andromache recovers herself sufficiently to turn her wrath upon Helen instead, whom she can curse without endangering her child's burial. Here it is open to us to conclude that to blame Helen is merely a reflex for those who dare not openly blame the Greeks; is it correct to find in Helen the source of all Andromache's woes or does that gesture, like that of the Greeks, target the innocent?

The speech takes a challenging turn towards the end, with a disruption in the metre at 774 that matches Andromache's terrible cries of 'Take him, carry him, throw him'. In 775 she proceeds to yet more fearful imperatives, enjoining the Greeks to 'feast on his flesh'. Given Andromache's earlier line about barbarian wrongs, it is provocative here to find the Trojan envisaging cannibalism, but projecting it onto Greeks as the logical conclusion of their conduct. It becomes perhaps more provocative when we realise that quite a few of the modern versions, discussed below, omit this line.

After the emotionally draining scene of Astyanax's departure, the chorus and Hekabe again react in different ways. At 792 Hekabe speaks of what can and cannot be done, repeating the lesson that Talthybios taught; she is ready to give up, following her own advice to Andromache. At this point the chorus takes over, singing a song in a completely different register from the scenes we have just witnessed (799-858). The description of Euripidean theatre as constantly changing tone and register used to be understood as a sign of dramatic incompetence, but a renewed appreciation of the performance dimension allows us to see it as a consummate skill in orchestrating audience response. Whatever the audience might expect next, this song's exquisite evocation of Salamis, the favoured youths of Troy, and the legendary history of its earlier destruction, is probably not it. Barlow's discussion emphasises the Pindaric metre and imagery, which she suggests contrast with its tone of despair. Inasmuch as Pindaric songs often relate a city's heroic present to its divinely favoured past, this ode is appropriate to an account of Troy, although it has to lament a disjunction between past and present rather than celebrating a continuity. Picked out for special glory as well as for special destruction, this version of Troy, we are reminded, may offer a possible paradigm for Athens.

Although the ode, beginning with Salamis, seems as if it will offer another list of places where the chorus might end up, it quickly moves on to the lord of Salamis, Telamon, who is a hero from the era before the Trojan War. Any notion of legendary heroic distance, however, is quickly lost in the misery of Troy's double destruction, by Herakles and then by Agamemnon, and is translated to the indifferent distance characteristic of those fortunate Trojans who have been removed to Olympus as beloved of the gods. The Sapphic language[39] in the song speaks of desire, but the ode concludes with a restatement of the distance between human and god, and even between ordinary humans and those selected for divine attention. While certain moments speak to harmonious relations between human and god, notably when Athena provides Athens with a *stephanos* of olive (803), the ode closes with the chorus only just restraining themselves from reproaching Zeus.

Helen

Helen is the third of the 'daughters' of Hekabe, and she too challenges the old queen with what seems at first an impossibly paradoxical argument. This scene is much commented in all the criticism, and several issues emerge repeatedly, in particular the sophistic quality of the argumentation and the moral standing of Hekabe.[40] Helen is particularly adept at exploiting the gap between the 'word' and the 'world', but Hekabe displays a surprising ability too.

The scene opens with the arrival of Menelaos and his cheerful apostrophe to the sun and the daylight (860). The jarring contrast in tone with the chorus's song is almost comical, as Menelaos proceeds blithely oblivious to the carnage and destruction all around him. Comical too is the combination of 862-3, in which he names Helen, and 869-70, in which he says he cannot bear to name his wife, but many editors excise the first couplet. The status of Helen is complex in Menelaos' speech, as well as in the ensuing scene; she is Menelaos' *damar* (866) the same word that Andromache used for her new status, and which is normally translated 'wife', but she is counted (872) among the Trojan prisoners. If the war was started by a woman's independent movement, it will nonetheless end with all the women including Helen being moved around at men's disposal. The Trojan women represent Helen as utterly separate from themselves, since she causes suffering and they suffer, but some critics consider that the play instead allows us to see that rather than distinct, the women are all connected by their subjugation to the male.[41]

Although the fate of Helen is allegedly at stake in this scene, there are in fact no dramatic developments. Since the Greek audience was aware that the *Odyssey* represents Helen and Menelaos as enjoying a (relatively) peaceful old age together in Sparta, it might wonder at the beginning of the scene if this play was going to change the myth – but it does not. Menelaos explains that Helen has been 'given' to him by the army (873) either to kill or to take home, and he has decided to have her killed at home, as repayment for the friends who lost their lives in Troy (878). At the end of the *agôn* between Helen and Hekabe, Menelaos leaves the stage ostensibly to take Helen home and execute her, so that like most Euripidean *agônes*, this contest between the two women changes nothing.[42]

Before Helen appears, Hekabe intercepts Menelaos with a prayer to Zeus, which is also obliquely addressed to the Greek leader (884-8). In this prayer she welcomes the advent of justice, which it seems that she identifies with the death of Helen. For a number of reasons, the prayer sits uncomfortably with the rest of Hekabe's discourse on deity. In attributing justice (888) to the gods she contradicts much that she has said so far, and it is not clear that she is correct here rather than anywhere else; rather than an acclamation of divine justice achieved, we should perhaps construe the speech as a plea to Menelaos for Helen's death. Another notable feature of this prayer is that it is couched in highly sophistic, fifth-century terms, the strangeness of which is immediately remarked upon by Menelaos (889). Quite traditional when she addresses Zeus as 'whoever you are, hard to know' (885), Hekabe then qualifies Zeus as (886) 'necessity of nature or mind of mortals'.[43] The terms *anagkê*,

necessity, *physis*, nature and *nous*, mind, are all foregrounded
in sophistic discourse, and although they are jarring here in the
speech of the elderly queen of Troy, they prepare for Helen's
highly sophistic argumentation, and even for elements of what
Hekabe will say.

At first, Hekabe tries to prevent any *agôn* happening, by
ensuring that Menelaos does not see Helen. She warns him of
the danger inherent in Helen, attributing to her alone the
destruction that has been wrought by Greeks (882). Helen has
kêlêmata, charms and bewitchment, that undermine reason,
but they have apparently blinded Hekabe too to the identity of
the aggressors. Hekabe's misrecognition of the Greeks extends
to her identifying herself with Menelaos in 894, and collapsing
the difference between Greeks and Trojans in 'those who have
suffered' (*hoi peponthotes*).

Enter Helen, well-dressed and coiffed, as Hekabe later com-
plains (1025-7), apparently calm and self-possessed.[44] Her first
move is to ask what has been decided about her life, and her
next is to ask for an opportunity to argue her defence (903-4).
Her self-consciousness about the staging of the *agôn* is not
unlike that of Kassandra when she moves out of 'madness' to
speak clearly (366-7), and of Andromache when she tells Hekabe that she has a 'most beautiful argument' (634-5). When
Menelaos repeats his determination to kill her (904), Hekabe
interrupts, invoking the 'justice' which she hopes will convict
Helen all the more thoroughly – although it may instead allow
her to escape. Menelaos' reaction can be understood as the first
of the denials of responsibility that will inform the *agôn*. Because Hekabe requests it, and because there is time, he permits
the *agôn*; he is not, by his own account, at all invested in what
is going on (911-14). Is there any real debate over Helen's future
or is Menelaos, his mind made up, indulging himself in a staged
catfight?[45]

As the defendant, Helen should speak second by the 'laws' of
the dramatic *agôn*, but as Lloyd points out no prosecution is
needed here, and in any case Helen swiftly turns into the
accuser – of Hekabe.[46] Blaming Hekabe, Priam and Menelaos

himself for instigating the strife at Troy, she claims complete innocence on her side. Hekabe is 'this woman here' (919), in the third rather than the second person, responsible first for giving birth to Paris and then with Priam culpable for not killing him immediately. Helen meanwhile, having unjustly lost her reputation, should in a perversion of Kassandra's paradox be crowned with a *stephanos* for her services to Greece (936).

To this opening Hekabe, as commentators note, offers no answer, as indeed she cannot, because it is an irrefutable argument, and the truth of it was demonstrated in the first play.[47] We have also seen Andromache blame Paris, the son of Hekabe, for the war, which is only one step away from blaming Hekabe herself. Helen is correct about other issues too; for instance she points, as part of her defence, to the fact that Greeks are not subject to barbarians, and all fifth-century Greeks knew that they were indeed free (932-4). Helen's next topic is more specific, and concerns the responsibilities of the gods. Since Aphrodite willed that Helen go with Paris, how could she have resisted? Menelaos needs to punish divinity, not his wife, if he wishes to apportion blame correctly (948). Again, since we have seen these gods, and since Hekabe has experienced them, it is difficult to see how we can find Helen anything but quite correct. Although her final point concerns what she did after Paris' death, and is contradicted by Hekabe, the play is silent as to which side has the right.

Helen's overall defence, then, is that she is responsible for nothing, and she assigns the blame for the Trojan War to almost anybody else. The paradoxical nature of her thesis aligns it with the arguments that the other 'daughters' of Hekabe have mounted, but her diagnosis is disturbingly accurate; to search closely for the source of the Trojan War is undoubtedly to find Hekabe and her son. Helen's discourse thus corresponds with the contemporary charge against the sophists, that they made the 'weaker' (morally) argument into the 'stronger' (rhetorically). The chorus recognise what is happening immediately, since they term the discourse '*peithô*', persuasion, and find it terrifying that one so evil should speak well (966-8). Those scholars like Lloyd who suggest that fifth-century sophistic discourse and the arguments of such as Gorgias are irrelevant to Helen here are more sanguine than the chorus.[48] By contrast, the chorus are so caught up by Helen's rhetoric that they call on Hekabe to defend her children and fatherland (966), even though she has neither. Recognising Helen's power, they also get the measure of its horror; how can she get off lightly over whom so much blood has been spilt, and conversely how can she who has suffered so much be the guilty party? Helen's demonstration that the quest for final guilt is illusory infuriates and frightens as much as did sophistic debates.[49] Even Dover, who argues cogently that responsibility for the Trojan War is shared among several characters, lists Helen, Paris, Priam, the Trojan people and the Greek commanders, without bringing himself to arraign Hekabe as well.[50]

To begin her reply, the prosecution speech against Helen and her own defence against the new charges, Hekabe announces that she will become an 'ally' to the goddesses and show that Helen is speaking what is not just (*endika*, 970). Although she has only recently noted how inadequate the gods are as allies, the overriding imperative to get Helen killed dictates another tack. Whether she has rediscovered her faith, or whether she invokes the deities in cynical opportunism, the fact that we have, as just noted, seen these gods, means that Hekabe's words are difficult to take at face value. The theatre of Euripides is distinguished by its unsparing dissection of the moment when the victim turns aggressor to exact revenge, confounding previous moral calculations; what is particularly intriguing here is that Hekabe will *not* clearly succeed in getting Helen killed, so that her revenge is incomplete and her compromises wasted.

As well as invoking questionable deities, Hekabe's revenge here requires that she identify wholeheartedly with the Greek conquerors. Helen had tried to forestall arguments that she imagined being made against her, but Hekabe goes one better and starts to talk like a Greek. She collapsed Trojan into Greek when she said to Menelaos 'you and me and all those who have suffered' (894); now she states that Hera and Athena could not be so stupid as to sell Argos to 'barbarians' or enslave Greeks to Phrygians (971-4). Whereas Andromache had equated Greeks to barbarians in order to convict them of the brutality of executing Astyanax, Hekabe willingly names herself a barbarian and denigrates her people – anything in order to see Helen's head on the plate. The dialectic of self and other, the rhetoric of sympathy and identification, mutate under pressure of this one end.

Hekabe goes still further in her rehabilitation of deity, as far indeed as to suggest that it barely exists at all. Since the story of the Judgement of Paris supports Helen's disreputable arguments, Hekabe contends that no such judgement took place (975-6).[51] At a stroke, she rewrites myth in such a way that history too would be altered, and her own status as a legendary figure severely compromised – a legendary figure whom she knows will be the subject of song in the future (1242-5). In this gesture she is like the many other Euripidean characters who cast doubt on the myths that they themselves inhabit, such as Helen in the prologue to *Helen* and Elektra in the recognition scene of *Elektra*.

While this intellectual gesture of doubting myths is very characteristic of sophistic debate, it is deployed here, paradoxically, in an attempt to defend deity. By denying the Judgement of Paris, Hekabe endeavours to prove that Helen alone was responsible for Helen's transgression, without the intervention of deity. Instead of divine intervention, Hekabe relies on the sophistic point that the words 'Aphrodite' and '*aphrosunê*' (mindlessness) begin with the same syllables, and thus that Helen's mind became Aphrodite.[52] Implicitly, then, Hekabe queries the ontological status of the gods and drifts towards the Protagorean argument that human beings constitute the only measure there is. Whereas Helen preserves a traditional attitude towards the gods and their untrammelled power to move human beings, even within the confines of her sophistic *peithô*, Hekabe, nominally defending them, ends up by implicitly questioning their existence. That the two women can exchange places in this fashion supports the overall contention of Helen's discourse that there is little point in pursuing the guilty, because like the victors and the vanquished, they have changed places with the innocent.

Hekabe continues her indictment of Helen by a variety of different arguments and by representing herself as varyingly Trojan or Greek. Thus Helen lays eyes on Paris 'shining in gold and barbarian clothes' (991-2) and Hekabe plays to the hilt the antithesis between the luxurious barbarian city and the poverty-stricken confines of Menelaos' Sparta (993-7). If this is a chance to dig at the Greeks, well and good, but it also seems to denigrate the barbarian Trojans by assimilating to them the depraved Helen. Countering the suggestion that Helen left Sparta against her own will (which Helen has not in fact made), Hekabe asks how come, when she cried out, nobody heard her – there was no dearth of strapping young men around to help (997-1000). Then, when she was in Troy, Helen was an opportunist who supported the winning side, whichever it was, and showed no loyalty to Greece of the kind that she has claimed (1002-9). She says she tried to escape, but when was she found trying to commit suicide, as a noble woman would, in longing for a former spouse (1010-14)? This suicide, if it had happened, would have been the opposite of Hekabe's advice to Andromache, when she counselled her daughter to make the best of her life with a new husband. Opposed again is the advice Hekabe represents herself as giving to Helen; she calls her 'daughter' and tries to help her escape, apparently without hatred (1015-19). It is open to us to conclude that the Trojan women are directing towards Helen the hatred that they dare not express towards the Greek men, and that the play exposes this self-delusion as sharply as it does any Greek atrocities. Helen, counter to all expectations, would then indeed be a victim as much as are the Trojan captives, and victory would perhaps look a lot like defeat.[53]

Critical opinion on Hekabe's speech is divided, especially over the last few lines. Several readers find that Hekabe throws away the moral high ground here with her accusations against Helen of coming before Menelaos in finery instead of with her head shaved and shivering in rags (1022-8).[54] Helen is perhaps the only Euripidean character who declines the trademark rags![55] Many also note that it is Helen's word against Hekabe's over whether or not she tried to escape, so that the 'truth' of the situation eludes us.[56] More striking perhaps than Helen's physical appearance is the distressing spectacle of Hekabe as she identifies – even if only strategically – so wholeheartedly with her conquerors. The *stephanos* passes to Menelaos and the Greeks (1030), and he is positioned to pass a *nomos*, a law, for all women, that they die if they betray their husbands (1031). Even fifth-century Athens did not go so far.[57]

The chorus join in enthusiastically with the appeal to execute Helen, citing Menelaos' ancestors, his house and his reputation in Greece – and even his reputation among his enemies (1033-5). When Helen's next gesture is more suitable to her situation, being a plea for forgiveness by Menelaos' knees, Hekabe intervenes on behalf of Greece's allies and their children – even though she knows by now how Greeks can treat children. Menelaos tries to assert control by ordering Helen to the ships, but even so he is forced to engage in further dialogue with Hekabe over the exact way in which Helen will travel. At 1049 Hekabe urges that Helen not be in the same ship, and Menelaos replies (1050) 'Why? Does she carry more weight than before?' Notorious for being a note of humour in an otherwise signally bleak exchange, this line has caused concern and even omission in some translations. An explanation of it in terms of superstitions about ships, rather than in terms of Helen's figure, is plausible,[58] but in any case the main point is that Menelaos misses the point, and refuses to acknowledge that the issue is his desire for his wife.

Who 'wins' the *agôn*? Commentators agree that normally the defendant speaks second, and wins, with stronger speech and more sympathetic character.[59] Although Helen is formally the defendant here, and speaks first, yet Hekabe is defending too, her children and country, the friends and country of Menelaos, and it is no easy matter to triumph over Helen's sophistic skill. But as we have seen, Hekabe is no mean sophist herself, so that the order of the speakers is not, here, a reliable guide to the victor. Some critics conclude that Hekabe wins because she is more rational,[60] or because she has more 'moral feeling, human sympathy and common sense'.[61] Others, as we have seen, conclude that Hekabe loses, because she gives up the moral high ground in her pursuit of Helen. Few fail to note that the Homeric *Odyssey* in any case tells us that Helen 'wins' the long game of survival.[62] Others respond appropriately to the sophistic conundrums by observing that the audience derive no secure impression of what will happen and cannot judge the right at all, particularly when the whole enterprise of searching out the guilty has come to seem thoroughly questionable.[63]

After Helen leaves, the only 'daughter' to exit to what may be a bearable future, the chorus sing their fourth song. So far the songs have described a trajectory that takes them further into the past history of the city as a whole; from the women's fears for their future in Greece they have moved to the night of the Wooden Horse and the love affairs between Olympus and Troy. The fourth song moves back again, beginning with the identity and history of Troy and subsequently focusing on the personal fates of the Trojan women, their dead husbands and the children they must abandon. In the last part of the song the chorus turns to Helen with curses on her and Menelaos, calling for a thunderbolt to strike their ship on the way home to Sparta. Now that Menelaos has gone, they can give their hatred free rein, and they are also outspoken in their accusations against the gods.

The chorus begin by indicting Zeus for the betrayal of Troy, and more particularly for the betrayal of his own temple and fragrant altar (1060-2). What is lost now is not so much the history of Troy as its naturally beautiful places, such as Mt Ida with its ivy covered glades, running with rivers of melted snow, a holy place where the edge catches the first light of day (1066-70). Nature joins with ritual observation as the other things lost (*phroudos*, 1071) are sacrifices, choruses, songs, all-night festivals, gods' statues and sacrificial moon-cakes. The pathetic repetitions in this song are notable, especially 'Ida, Ida'

71

(1066) and 'I care, I care whether you think of this' (1077). This last is directed to Zeus, who is imagined sitting on a heavenly throne in the *aithêr* above the burning city, fatefully involved with, and horribly separate from, the humans.

The chorus's question is perhaps answered in the rest of the song. The husband wanders unburied while the woman is taken by a swift ship to Argos (1081-8). Meanwhile the children are separated from their mothers and cry out (1090, with another pathetic repetition), calling their mothers and lamenting that they are carried off alone. The Greek word for alone is *monan*, with a feminine ending, because all the males of Troy are dead, reminding us perhaps that the girl like her mother will be sexually exploited and never become the *parthenos* of 1107, who is compared to Helen in her delight in golden mirrors. The child's lament tails off strangely, listing the places that she might go to in Greece, rather as her mother did in the first song.

Astyanax

If we recall the sacrificial deaths of the sister of the Heraclids in *Children of Herakles*, and the son of Creon in *Phoenician Women*, we may not expect to see Astyanax again. Those who died quietly for their families or cities are not remembered subsequently by their respective plays. But in a coup of theatrical brilliance we do see Astyanax, laid out on his father's shield. Although the death is not strictly speaking sacrificial, the leap from the city walls of the young king, last remaining descendant of Priam, has unmistakable sacrificial contours. The dead boy is also a warrior, fallen for the city and borne in on the shield he would inherit, and laid to rest by the hands of the women who loved him, in the way that Kassandra described for all the Trojan fallen (390). Lastly he is a *diskêma pikron* (1121), literally a bitter discus, evoking the realm of aristocratic sporting activity that he will not inherit, and perhaps reminiscent too of childhood games.

Talthybios makes his penultimate appearance with the body on the shield. He addresses Hekabe informally (1123), as he did at the start of the play, and very differently from how he addressed Andromache when he had to bring the news of her son's condemnation. Even if we represent him as sympathetic, he does not immediately discourse of Astyanax, because he is more interested in the Greeks' misfortunes than in those of the Trojans. Echoing the words of the chorus about disasters come upon the land (1118-19), Talthybios explains that Neoptolemos has left because his grandfather, the father of Achilles, is under attack by the son of Pelias. If this development is, as editors conclude, a Euripidean invention, it indicates that the bitter homecoming for the Greeks is already taking effect; and the word with which Talthybios describes Neoptolemos, *phroudos* (1130), gone, vanished, is exactly the word that has repeatedly been deployed by the Trojans to describe their lives. Talthybios' speech is of interest in other ways too. Andromache, to the last, did not curse the Greeks, but she was not able to bury her son because of her new lord's hasty departure. However, she has pleaded successfully with Neoptolemos for her son to be buried by the other women, and she has also obtained a reprieve for the shield of Hektor, which will receive the body of Astyanax and not hang, a ghastly memento, in her new marriage chamber (1133-42). Lee notes that the lines in which Talthybios describes the shield and Andromache's requests are not among Euripides' best, but any awkwardness may be attributed to Talthybios' embarrassment at what he has to say. Thus Lee remarks that *pesôn* (1134), falling, is deployed as the passive of *rhiptô*, I throw, but perhaps this is because the herald was reluctant to say 'being thrown'.[64] Talthybios then moves to discuss the shield of Hektor, but his first words, 'fear of the Achaeans' (1136), might also seem fleetingly to refer to *nekron tode* (1134), this corpse, especially since Hekabe will make the point that Astyanax dies because the Greeks are afraid of him (1190-1). Although the burial cannot be elaborate because the Greeks are in haste to leave (1148), Astyanax will still receive the *stephanos* (1144). Whether Talthybios washes the corpse in order to speed the process, or because of a human sympathy of which he has shown symptoms, he ends his speech on a note of cooperation between Greeks and Trojans which is more positive than Hekabe's earlier identification with the avenging conquerors. Yet at the same time he speaks with blithe unfeeling of the Trojans going 'home' (1155).

The three scenes with her 'daughters' each required a complex response from Hekabe, but her grandson evokes a single long speech of mourning which also becomes, by reason of its positioning towards the close of the play, a farewell to the earth and the city. In this moving piece of theatre the dramatist out-Euripidises Euripides; of all the children in his extant plays pitifully parted from their parents and lamentably dying, none receives a funeral oration except Astyanax.[65] The forerunners are no longer Homer, Aeschylus or the sophists but the most tragic of playwrights himself, at the top of his game.[66] Critics are unanimous that this is Greek tragedy's 'most distressing moment',[67] a scene of 'unsurpassed bleakness' which at the same time is 'the product of one of Euripides' richest poetic ideas'.[68] The visible paradox of child and shield both epitomises and exceeds all the play's other paradoxes. Yet the scene may also remind us that while this child must die, another child – Paris – did not die, and the guilt of that omission, which helped to lead to the Trojan War, may be thought as culpable as the guilt of this Greek commission.

Showcasing Hekabe's rhetorical skill, the virtuoso scene also draws on her position as sometime queen of Troy and her role as grandmother. To the last a leader of her community, she improvises mourning for Astyanax and puts together a ritual from whatever she has left.[69] That it is not the mother who laments the child is part of the grim irony of Astyanax's death, which replays the trope of the young dying and the old burying them, but at a distance of two generations instead of one. At 1229 the chorus even address Hekabe as 'mother'. The paradoxical structure of this bereavement is reinforced by the notion that Astyanax dies because the Greeks are afraid of him – yet how can massed adult warriors fear a child? Hekabe's funeral speech brilliantly has it both ways, because on the one hand it emphasises the pity of the premature death with the various tropes of childhood, like the lost sleep of the watching carer (1187-8), but on the other it collects references to what Astyanax would have been, an adult Trojan male and thus a threat to the Greeks – as Hekabe herself had suggested to Andromache – and so is part of regular heroic discourse. Thus the speech dwells on the tropes of successful youth, like sporting triumphs, a bride and regal power (1168-70), but at the same time addresses the different parts of the infant body (1175-9).[70] As Segal puts it, 'Instead of conferring immortal fame on a great warrior by eulogising his deeds, [Hekabe] checks the movement towards transcendence by enacting the archetypal role of the *mater dolorosa* over a dead child'.[71] The pathos increases when the voice of Astyanax is heard in the speech (1182-4) and yet there is also a fascinating disjunction, because the child who was apparently very young in the scene with Andromache, cowering at his mother's breast, is now old enough to address his grandmother authoritatively, discussing her funeral and his role in it.[72]

The funeral speech points up the sadness of Astyanax's death by contrasting with his vulnerability two inanimate objects that outlast him. Hekabe quotes not only his speech but also his imagined, paradoxical epitaph – a child killed by Greeks who feared him – which preserves simultaneously his memory and the shame of the Greeks (1190-1). What is more pathetic and paradoxical is that there will not be an epitaph at all; this inanimate object remains imaginary, and Astyanax is consigned to an unmarked grave. The second object is the shield of Hektor, in which Astyanax is to be buried and to which Hekabe addresses the latter part of her speech. As commentators have noted, this shield is itself a paradox because while it will not die with Astyanax even though it will be buried, all the lasting physical traces which it bears upon its surface are signs of absence. It will gain honours and the *stephanos* (1123) but its glory was Hektor, and its significance is the absence of Hektor. Segal's account is exemplary:[73]

Everything in this ritual is a figure of absence and enacts the paradox of embodied absence ... The shield that serves as Astyanax's coffin is also a figure for Hector's absence. The impress of his right hand on the leather strap is the visible symbol of the body that is not there. The sweat that dripped into the shield reminds us both of his mortality and of the failure of those 'toilsome efforts' (*ponoi*) from which the sweat flowed. Even the 'beard' reminds us of the nonadolescence of Astyanax, of the truncated life cycle of the son who, though buried in the father's shield, will not grow up to be like his father.

The shield thus equivocates between the physical and the imaginary, a compelling image of the misfit between language and the world. In its ironic bid for immortality it perhaps foreshadows what Hekabe will subsequently say about the poetic survival of Troy. Emerging from the lyrical lamentation that she shares with the chorus, after her funeral speech, she reflects that if the gods had not turned Troy upside down, Trojans would not be a matter of song for future generations (1242-5). While this utterance suggests that she can stand outside her present moment, and even envisage a future, it also aligns her with Helen in *Iliad* 6, who knows that she and Paris provide topics for future songs, and thus repeats the gesture that the play has made elsewhere, of undermining the differences between Greek and Trojan, victory and defeat.

If the opening of the play was a kind of endgame, as Dunn suggests in *Tragedy's End*, there is little surprise in the fact that much of the ending repeats elements of the beginning.[74] Hekabe was on the ground then and is so now, although here she and the women are beating the ground in an attempt to communicate with their dead; Troy was no more then and is no more now (99-100, 1292). The logical consequences of the fall of Troy have worked themselves out and Troy now falls conclusively, in flames. Other elements of the ending, however, as Dunn also notes, frustrate the conventions of Greek tragedy, and thus obviate any consoling sense of closure. When the chorus women see torches on the walls of Troy, our experience of similar moments might make us expect a *deus ex machina* —

but as we have seen, no *deus* ever comes. The play offers a series of appropriate closing gestures and closes with none; thus Hekabe tries to run into the flames of Troy, committing the suicide that Talthybios found proper, but is prevented, so must find another way to end the drama.[75] Similarly, once Hekabe has announced that the name of Troy will last in song, she goes on to contradict herself (1277-8), and the chorus women twice lament that the name will disappear (1319, 1322). It is thus not clear that we can straightforwardly celebrate Troy's 'eternal spirit' as David Stuttard, for example, bids us do.[76] As in *Iphigeneia at Aulis*, where we are almost offered the choice, at the close of the play, of Iphigeneia rescued by Artemis or of Iphigeneia dead and the rescue a consoling fiction,[77] so here we are still confronted, right to the very end, with the possibility of concluding with hope or with despair.

A close reading of the play as it unfolds compels us to acknowledge its relentless dramatic and emotional energy. Far from static or undeveloped, *Trojan Women* is dynamically theatrical, harnessing varied and intense audience responses with consummate skill. From the constant presence of Hekabe, through the impassioned dance of Kassandra, to the stillness of Astyanax, it is correspondingly demanding on the stamina and technique of actors. Over and above this, it is penetratingly intelligent, dissecting the extremes of situation and behaviour and grimly engrossed by the paradoxes that they generate. Divine and mortal, male and female, victor and vanquished, Greek and barbarian, guilty and innocent, are sifted through its series of perverse speeches and surprising actions, and none emerges unscathed. Testimony to this intelligence is the abiding engagement of audiences and readers in the processes of moral evaluation that the play renders so necessary and so difficult.

3

Twentieth-century
Receptions

I shall consider here some of the major versions of *Trojan Women* from the second half of the twentieth century, when, as indicated earlier, *Trojan Women* achieved critical recognition both as literary drama and as script for theatrical performance.[1] Guided by the new plays themselves, my particular topics of discussion will alter from one play to the next, but I will have occasion to note the variations on certain themes such as justice, the role of the divine, the guilt of Helen, the strength of Hekabe, the death of Astyanax, and what I have called 'Kassandra's paradox' about victory and defeat. Although there have been several important productions of *Trojan Women* in the twentieth century, I have concentrated here on published versions, in order that my readings can be assessed independently by other readers.[2]

As we noted earlier, the perceived nature of the wars in the second half of the last century, deliberately targeting civilians, seems to have led audiences and readers to a new relationship to *Trojan Women*. In the context of nuclear conflict, moreover, invoked by Sartre and Harrison, the work of rediscovery seems more urgent in that war threatens even its own literary commemoration. Along with a renewed critique of warfare goes a much greater emphasis on the enduring conflict between male and female, which is a part of *Trojan Women*, but to a comparatively understated extent. This issue is perhaps particularly compelling in Kennelly, Mee, and the film and theatre productions that we shall consider. While these versions foreground male aggression against women, they also meditate on the capacity of women for violence, which is further underlined in McLaughlin. At the beginning of the new century, Osofisan's play *The Women of Owu* returns to the issues of guilt and responsibility, staging events very similar to those of the Greek play but opening them up to diametrically opposed interpretations.

Before we consider the versions of the second half of the century, however, we should recall that Gilbert Murray's translation, and the associated productions in the early years of the century, were instrumental in sparking a revival of interest in Euripides after the nineteenth century had condemned his work as rhetorical and incompetent.[3] They also fixed the notion of *Trojan Women* as anti-war.[4] The translation was produced for the theatre numerous times in Britain and America, largely by Hartley Granville-Barker or Maurice Browne, from 1905 until after World War I. At its inception, Murray saw it as part of a protest against the Boer War; at other moments in its production history the sufferings of the play were aligned with those of the victims of the Great War, as when the news of the sinking of the *Lusitania*, in 1915, was announced on stage with the words 'This play is about a deed like that'.[5] Hartigan stresses how these productions made Greek tragedy seem live and relevant to contemporary politics; she also shows how revolutionary were the choices to stage the play in sports stadiums and music halls.[6] Sybil Thorndike memorably recorded an encounter with an 'old barrow-woman neighbour' who had got the full measure of the play's contemporary significance:

> Well dearie, we saw your play, it was lovely; and we all 'ad a good cry and a nice walk 'ome over the bridge and shrimps for tea – You see them Trojans was just like us, we've lost our sons and 'usbands in this bleedin' war, 'aven't we, so no wonder we was all cryin' – that was a real play, that was, dearie.

Murray found this reaction 'another score for Euripides'.[7] The first notable translation and performances since antiquity, then, gathered together a series of themes that we shall encounter again, such as the innovative use of theatre resources and the inescapable, living force of the tragedy.

Sartre, *Les Troyennes*

The Oxford Archive of Performances of Greek and Roman Drama shows at least one performance of *Trojan Women* in English, amateur or professional, for every year between World Wars I and II.[8] Although Hartigan suggests that *Trojan Women* was not commercially popular in the USA during the 1950s,[9] a series of accessible translations ensured that the play was occasionally performed in various Anglophone countries and in continental Europe, while in France it gave rise to an important adaptation by Jean-Paul Sartre. Directed by Cacoyannis for the Théâtre Nationale Populaire in 1965, it was Sartre's last play.[10] At the time the choice of *Trojan Women*, what Bernard Pingaud in the 'Introduction' to the published English language version calls 'the most static and the least theatrical' of the Greek plays – an 'oratorio' rather than a drama – might seem perverse (vii, xii).[11] Sartre's explanation of his decision is relevant to us because it is as much about the relations of a mid-twentieth-century audience to an ancient Greek play as it is about the play itself. The exposition begins by claiming that Euripides was using a convention to destroy a convention; that is, he was writing in traditional mode for people who were beginning to criticise traditional assumptions, or, in Sartre's words, 'were listening to characters who had beliefs which they no longer held themselves' (ix). This kind of disjunction makes the task of the translator more difficult, since he is already dealing with the problem of the disjunction between then and now; 'how to bridge the gap which separates the [contemporary] audience from the climate of opinion that obtained when the plays were written' (ix).[12] Although this problem is especially acute in relation to the gods, Sartre claims to be able to do little other than restate Euripides' position on them because he had to 'construct some of the conformity of belief before I could, as it were, destroy it' (xiii-xiv, x). In certain respects, however, the

80

gods of the Greek play assist the work of the French philoso-
pher, because in eventually rejecting the humans, these gods
force the humans to acknowledge 'their own death' and thus
open for them the possibility of realising the necessity of exis-
tentialism. This is, however, the only note of possibility in the
ending which is otherwise 'total nihilism' (xv).[13]

In the light of these difficulties, Sartre explains that he
adapted rather than simply translating, by which he seems to
mean that he made certain specific adjustments such as explaining allusions and increasing the moments of dramatic
tension (xi-xii). Once these adjustments have been discussed,
however, the Introduction moves to a meatier topic, namely the
subject matter of the play. Despite all the difficulties of cultural
background and climate of opinion, the subject matter alone
justifies the otherwise perverse choice of play, because the play
is about war. The war in question, however, seems to shift as
the Introduction proceeds. Apparently, Sartre's interest in *Trojan Women* is kindled by a faithful translation staged by
Jacqueline Moatti during the 'Algerian War' (xii). The Algerian
War is here the name for the Algerians' struggle against French
colonial occupation, one of the more horrific post-imperial contests which involved the systematic use of torture and which
was therefore condemned by many French intellectuals, including Sartre.[14] Acknowledging this 'colonial war' further, and very
likely extending its reference to French Indo-China or Vietnam,
Sartre explains that his use of the term 'Europe' in the play,
while an anachronism, is allowable because (xiii)

it is the equivalent of the ancient antagonism which ex-
isted between the Greeks and the barbarians, that is,
between Greece and the civilization around the Mediter-
ranean, and the gradual infiltration into Asia Minor
where colonial imperialism arose. It was this colonialism
of Greece into Asia Minor that Euripides denounced, and
where I use the expression 'dirty war' in reference to these
expeditions I was, in fact, taking no liberties with the
original text.

81

While Sartre thus constructs an equivalence between Greek colonisation of Asia Minor and French imperialism in Algeria and elsewhere, he also wants to modulate this debate to a denunciation of war in general and nuclear war in particular. In the context of possible nuclear destruction, the identity between victor and vanquished that *Trojan Women* posits becomes relevant indeed. Sartre recruits Euripides thus (xii-xiii):

> The play had a precise political significance when it was first produced. It was an explicit condemnation of war in general and of imperial expeditions in particular. We know today that war would trigger off an atomic war in which there would be neither victor nor vanquished. The play demonstrates this fact precisely: that war is a defeat to humanity. The Greeks destroy Troy but they receive no benefit from their victory.

The specifics of the French's own 'imperial expeditions' give way to a more general fear of nuclear war.

In this context Sartre's reinsertion of Poseidon at the end of the play, as the *deus ex machina* which Euripides uncharacteristically denied himself, is even more intriguing.[15] Poseidon closes the play by explaining Hekabe's future (79) – though not her metamorphosis into a dog – and then announces more generally (80):

> We'll make you pay for this.
> You stupid, bestial mortals
> Making war, burning cities,
> Violating tombs and temples
> Torturing your enemies,
> Bringing suffering on yourselves.
> Can't you see
> War
> Will kill you:
> All of you?

The notion that 'war will kill all of you' returns us to Kassandra's paradox of victory and defeat, and corresponds to the realisation that in the nuclear winter neither victor nor vanquished will be at all. But in the colonial context, which is so clearly invoked elsewhere in the play, it is not simply the case that war killed all; what war did, in Algeria and later on in Vietnam, was drive out the French.[16] Despite the well-established credentials of Sartre's anti-colonial politics, the rejection of war here also serves to collapse European imperialism into a general condemnation of 'war'. We shall see again a tendency to collapse all wars into one, licensed by *Trojan Women*'s own collapse of the Trojan into the Peloponnesian War, but repeatedly problematic nonetheless.

That said, Sartre's drama is very clear-sighted about the failures of the colonial project. The lines that Sartre identifies as an interpolation on the theme of 'Europe' come directly after the departure of Astyanax to his death, so the irony of the Greek-drawn contrast between Greek and barbarian is all the more savage. The chorus begin their song by recalling an earlier Greek invasion of Troy, launched from Salamis. This notion combines the mythical many destructions of Troy with the historical Greek defeat of the Persians (not, crucially, a colonial venture). But the immediate surfacing of the colonial discourse of 'progress' and 'backwardness' lets us see that we are concerned with contemporary aggressions too, and the song becomes more explicit in its indictment (49):

> They told us then that they were bringing
> Greek culture and European enlightenment
> To the backward people of Asia:
> Our city burned with progress,
> Our young men had their limbs
> Amputated by philosophy.

While 'Our city burned with progress' may be ambiguous, 'Our young men had their limbs/amputated by philosophy' is less so. Similarly pungent are Talthybios' lines explaining how the

Greeks allowed Astyanax to be buried in his father's shield. To have the shield hanging in Neoptolemos' house for Andromache to see 'would have been cruel,/And we Europeans are both civilized/and sensitive' (71). Even Cassandra's account of how Greeks will die is subtly assimilated to the mid-twentieth-century colonial context, since the Greeks as they leave Troy will not be shipwrecked, but swallowed up by a foreign land, to die without leaving a trace (28).

The translator Duncan's version of the death of Astyanax marks a considerable divergence from Sartre's, which he is ostensibly translating. Andromache refuses to hand her son over to the Greeks immediately, but does not launch into a speech on motherhood. Instead, the stage directions have her holding his hands, fondling eyes and mouth in sequence as Hekabe does later.[17] Her outburst to the Greeks dehumanises Astyanax as it did in Euripides, but without the note of cannibalism. Duncan omits from his translation Andromache's accusation against the Greeks of barbarism, which is more developed in Sartre than in the Greek (81 in Sartre, *Les Troyennes*):

Men of Europe
You despise Africa and Asia,
And you call us barbarians, I think.
But when vain-glory and lust
Throw you into our homes
You pillage, you torture, you massacre.
Where are the barbarians then?
And you, the Greeks, so proud of your humanity,
Where are you?
I tell you: not one of us
Would have dared do to a mother
What you have done to me.

The probing of the victors' claims to civilisation is made more pointed by the colonial context.

The Greeks, however, or at least one of them, acts out a kind of compassion which is also an interpolation by Duncan. Astyanax holds a basket of seashells, perhaps to be read as a sign of Troy's coastal power, or perhaps an indication that with childish obliviousness he picks up shells on the beach where the enslaved women are waiting. He drops his basket as he is led off – we are not told if in fear or haste – and the solder who is taking him away to execution stops to pick the shells up and put them back in the basket (48). While there is perhaps an element of sentimentality in this interpolated moment, it may be recuperated within a larger argument. Leonard analyses Sartre's *Trojan Women* as questioning whether, in the face of colonial conflict and the possibility of nuclear war, there is any place for a traditional, Western, classically-inflected humanism. This act by the soldier, touching and futile in equal measure, gestures towards the humanist belief in a final redemption, but shows up the scale of the horrors even as it palliates them.[18]

Michael Cacoyannis, *Trojan Women*

Sartre's politically aware translation, which went beyond that of Murray in making quite explicit references to contemporary colonial struggles, provided a licence for subsequent adaptations set in the context of other twentieth-century agonies.[19] While *Trojan Women* has most often been called upon to denigrate types of armed conflict, including the colonial and the nuclear, some adaptations have focused on the struggle between male and female, as we shall see below. The Trojan women have been captured and enslaved in different cities across Europe, Asia, Africa and the Middle East, with varying degrees of masculine brutality. Other adaptations have eschewed specific reference and have let the action and characters speak to particular situations only through their general qualities of suffering and resistance. Not that this has necessarily protected them from the attentions of the constituted powers; the film of *Trojan Women* by the Greek director Michael Cacoyannis was banned by the military junta that ruled Greece in the 1970s. The APGRD database indicates that *Trojan Women* contributed to the resistance to the colonels in other ways, since

the translation by the Marxist poet Kostas Varnalis was performed in 1966 and 1971, and since excerpts from the play were
performed at 'An Evening of Free Greek Music and Drama'
sponsored by the Greek Committee against Dictatorship.

Completed in 1971, Cacoyannis' film is famous in part at
least for its star-studded cast: Katherine Hepburn played Hekabe, Irene Pappas Helen, Vanessa Redgrave Andromache and
Genevieve Bujold Kassandra. In a naturalistic style and an
outdoor location in Spain, the film makes no overt references to
politics in Greece or anywhere else. There are no gods, although
there is an introductory voice-over that tells the coming fate of
the Greeks. Despite its gleaming classical pedigree and international cast, however, the overall political attitude of the play
and its director led to the ban; the film concerns itself throughout with oppression and resistance, which were relevant in the
context of Vietnam and of the political upheaval in Paris in 1968
as well as of the Greek junta. Thus the women are much more
physically brutalised than is required by the Greek original,
being regularly pushed about and beaten by the soldiers. Nev-
ertheless, their collective actions continue to resist, and thus
implicitly valorise the expression of dissent.

On occasion the collective actions are directed against Helen
rather than the soldiers. The Helen scene is notable not so much
for any debate between her and Hekabe as for the fact that she
is brought in caged in a cart, probably in order to protect her
from the anger of the women, and that she openly invites that
anger when she bathes, naked, in the water that the captured
women are desperate to drink. Even apart from this scene, the
camera rejoices in Helen's sexuality and in her overt seduction
of Menelaos, over whom she finally triumphs, more by the
deployment of her body than by her words.[20] Several critics
comment that the film is not quite a film, because it retains too
much theatrical quality and does not always fully use the
resources of the cinema. When it does, as when the camera falls
from the battlements with Astyanax, giving us his view of his
death, it is typed as 'atrocious'.[21] Overall, critics found that the
film flattened out some of the differences among the four main

female characters, and sacrificed some of the Greek play's ambiguity.[22] It is not as pointed as some of the published adaptations that we shall go on to discuss, nor as experimental as some of the significant theatrical productions of recent years. That it had to be banned, however, despite its identity as part of the respected 'classical tradition', suggests again the disturbing force of the tragedy.

Andrei Serban, *Fragments of a Greek Trilogy*, and Tadashi Suzuki, *Trojan Women*

During the era of Vietnam, performances of *Trojan Women* could explicitly express dissent, as with the production by the Theater of the Lost Continent whose poster features a 70s peace emblem.[23] Two particular productions which emerged first in the 1970s have been since hailed as defining theatrical events of the second half of the twentieth century; they acknowledge their roots by responding not so much to the contemporary military conflict as to the accompanying sense, in the United States and elsewhere, of social breakdown and fragmentation. The productions by Serban and Suzuki, based on *Trojan Women*, each had a touring life of over ten years, with long runs in the first production space and extensive subsequent international tours. Both were international in other senses, in that they combined performance styles and theatrical traditions from various cultures, working variations on the Greek play's discourse of Greek and barbarian. Both were characterised as avant-garde, especially since they aimed not so much for a thought-provoking interpretive experience as for a visceral plunging into the extreme resources of the theatre, such as vocal music, stylised gesture, and anomalous or ritualised use of performance space. As such, they both departed far from the text of *Trojan Women* in its Greek or its later versions, while retaining the focus on suffering and the power to move an audience.

In its mature form, Andrei Serban's *Fragments of a Greek Trilogy* consisted of elements of *Medea, Elektra* and *Trojan*

Women, the last especially in a radically altered version. Devised initially in 1974 at La MaMa Annexe in New York, *Trojan Women* occupied the performance space in such a fashion that the audience members were herded round the auditorium by the actors in order to get out of the way of the action as it moved from one end of the space to the other. The varying emotional distance between actors and audience, which has concerned us at several points in this analysis, is here almost abolished. The audience was also subjected to an unusual auditory experience, since the production used numerous different languages, including Latin, Greek, African and pre-Columbian languages, as well as a range of non-linguistic hisses, clicks, and trills, to produce an aural environment that promoted emotional rather than intellectual response. The percussive music by Elizabeth Swados provided the guide for the audience's responses, and was itself composed from numerous different musical traditions.[24] Within these contexts the production afforded, as the awe-struck commentators all confirm, an almost unbearable degree of pity, terror, and raw human passion. As Avery Willis writes, there is no discourse, no realised characters, just relentless forms of action.[25] A number of scenes were devised that have only approximate equivalents in *Trojan Women*. Helen is brought into the performance space bound, then stripped naked, smeared with mud, loaded into a caged cart, and raped by a bear, amid triumphant cries from the captive women. Astyanax is lovingly prepared for death by his mother, who washes, anoints and dresses him while breathing incomprehensible words in the ancient languages and uttering a 'high-pitched, vibrato plaint'.[26] He is taken away in another cage, while his mother jumps to *her* death. At the close of the play the women try to escape, running up a ramp, only to be each hurled down again by the soldiers. They finally depart from the action in a 'ship' that is made up of their own chained, swaying bodies. Amy Green writes that 'Precision, simplicity, and hypnotic concentration joined in a disciplined technique that grounded the performers so securely to physical tasks that they were free to release an almost frightening, primordial emotional energy'.[27]

3. Twentieth-century Receptions

For our purposes, the varied and sometimes distant relations to the Euripidean *Trojan Women* are of particular interest. Without an explicit connection to a specific contemporary conflict, the production seems to foreground instead the hostility between the genders and the brutalisation of the women by the male victors. In this respect it may be seen to follow the lead of the Cacoyannis, which itself develops into a fully-fledged theme what was more implicit in *Trojan Women*. Other arguments canvassed by the Greek *Trojan Women* – about victory and defeat, Greek and barbarian, guilt and innocence – seem less central than the uncompromising representations of victimised suffering.

Commentators responded in similar terms to the *Trojan Women* of Tadashi Suzuki, which also drew on the resources of the body and of verbal music to deliver an unforgettable theatrical and emotional experience. The Suzuki production of *Trojan Women* underwent several changes in its fifteen-year international life, but commentators identify as its core concept a shell-shocked Old Man or Old Woman, who is located in a ruined cemetery, in what is apparently the aftermath of nuclear destruction, and who dreams of the Trojan women, in particular of Hekabe. Within these parameters, the text of the Greek *Trojan Women* is in large part jettisoned, the action being composed of 'the fragments in which the characters lay bare their feelings',[28] and the dialogue being minimal, composed of monologues and incantations.[29] Modern Japanese poetry by Makoto Ooka contributes to the fusion of styles from diverse performance traditions, including all the varieties of Japanese theatre which are usually kept apart from one another.[30]

The production dispenses with Helen and the Greek gods. The Japanese god Jizo stands impassive above the action throughout, the actor in question keeping perfectly still, until the very last moment when the god bends down towards the earth and the remaining characters, in a physically demanding feat of slow-motion. A series of ritualised, terrifying episodes unfolds, such as the on-stage rape of Andromache, and the death of Astyanax, which is accomplished by laughing samurai

89

dismembering a rag doll. Hekabe laments over the body before the entrance of Menelaos, who flies into a rage at the mere mention of Helen's name and sets about him, killing all the chorus members. The ending of the play took various forms but usually involved some kind of return to the 'present', to the Old Woman, a young girl victimised by Occupation troops, or modern-day tourists, and the musical accompaniment of a modern Japanese pop-song. Commentators stress the visceral, draining effect of this production rather than its argumentative structure, but the production would seem to have made a link between the catastrophe of nuclear war and the more generalised brutality of men to women. Similarly, the implicit critique of Allied bombing of Japan may be thought to evoke the contrasts in the Greek *Trojan Women* between Greek and barbarian.

Since there is much less discussion among the characters of the play than in the Greek, it is not easy to discern Kassandra's paradox at work, either in the Suzuki or indeed in the Serban. Victims and victors do not offer to change places as strikingly as they do in the Greek play, in part perhaps because they are securely identified as female and male, and without the gods' promises of shipwreck there is little point in speculating on the imminent downfall of the aggressors. It is of course open to us to read the downfall of the victorious 'Greeks' simply in the inhuman extremity of their violence. In the Greek *Trojan Women* there are no scenes of rape, dismemberment, or forced embarkation, and this difference points not simply to the conventional decorum of Athenian tragedy regarding events on-stage. It may also suggest that the Greek play is committed not simply to exposing war's pitiful scenes, but also to following the logic of its paradoxes.

Both these theatrical productions followed something of the lead of Euripides' *Trojan Women* in that they proved vehicles for virtuoso performers. In the Serban, the work of Priscilla Smith as Andromache drew unanimous praise, and in the case of the Suzuki, Shiraishi Kayoko astonished audiences by playing three different characters in each performance. It was partly the extraordinary skill of these actors that helped the productions to their iconic status. In general, these two productions were received as signifying a rediscovery of the visceral, emotive power of theatre, and especially of its ritual dimension. In these respects the productions can be seen to respond to some of the significant dimensions of *Trojan Women*, but in other ways they may work against the Greek play. For instance, neither production foregrounded the actual discursive work of language, demonstrating instead that theatre can communicate and unite without linguistic intelligibility.[31] In the analysis offered here, conversely, I have stressed the discursive and argumentative content of *Trojan Women*. Overall, commentators suggest that the productions of Serban and Suzuki seize on certain readily transferable aspects of *Trojan Women* to the exclusion of others. Of Serban, one critic writes 'For the New York production Euripides's text provided images and characters, amplified and expanded in the rehearsal process to become a blending of languages, cultures, races and even species in the service of Artaud's theatre of cruelty.'[32] Carruthers suggests that the innovative effects achieved by Serban and Suzuki were facilitated because the Greek *Trojan Women* has no plot.[33] Although *Trojan Women* does have a certain linearity, I for one might not agree with this claim, and in any case our response to *Trojan Women* is not therefore straightforward. From another perspective, even partial versions of *Trojan Women* testify to the sheer creativity of the play. Hartigan, for instance, writes that few dramas could sustain such alteration as is offered by the two productions discussed here, 'but the power of this play endures'.[34] This claim is amply borne out by all the receptions discussed here.

Tony Harrison, *Common Chorus II*

Many productions of *Trojan Women* in the late twentieth century moved audiences profoundly, especially when the production seemed, as perhaps those of Suzuki and Serban did not, to identify a contemporary conflict. In Israel in 1983 the production by the Habimah National Theatre resonated thus:[35]

Where one might expect to find solace, Israeli theatre doses its public with wormwood and gall. Sartre's *Trojan Women,* for example, was set in a [Palestinian] refugee camp with the guards wearing Israeli uniforms and carrying Israeli weapons. This was not a random choice for dramatic updating, but was staged during the turmoil that followed charges of Israeli negligence in permitting Phalangist massacres in Lebanon's Sabra and Shatila refugee camps. 'It was very hard to take, but it had some truth in it,' said actor Misha Asherov. To make a play of the past come to grips with the present is hardly a new idea; but methodically to create a setting with the intent of affronting the audience is not simply 'relevant,' to use a word with hackneyed overtones; it is provocative. It is a theatre of confrontation.

The confrontation is further explained by the actor Asherov:[36]

As I told you about *The Trojan Women,* if you play it in Athens or Troy in that time, what do you care about it? But if things [are represented], actual things that happen to you now, and you have to give the answers now, it turns the theatre ... the theatre becomes a live theatre.

Accounts of such productions repeat the theme of *Trojan Women*'s uncanny ability to transcend history and geography with its abhorrence of war, but the productions bring their own historical specificity, with their own identification of victims and victors that is then overturned.

Yet some politically engaged versions seem to import their specificities in less compelling fashion. Tony Harrison's version of *Trojan Women, The Common Chorus Part II*, which has its own political allegiances, has never been performed; *The Common Chorus Part I*, a rewriting of *Lysistrata*, has been performed by amateurs but not by professionals.[37] Such neglect is surprising, given Harrison's stature as one of Britain's foremost poets, but his introduction to the plays, published together for the first time in 2002 along with his translation of the *Oresteia*, supplies one explanation. The plays responded to the siting of American Cruise missiles at the United States Air Force base at Greenham Common during the 80s and 90s, and to the Women's Peace Camp which grew up around the gates of the base and which mounted a ceaseless protest against the threat of nuclear war, often taking very innovative forms, for nearly twenty years. When the Cold War ended and the missiles were returned to the States, the plays were 'marooned in their moment' – the missiles left behind Common and *Common Chorus* alike.[38]

While Harrison's introduction meditates on the necessary connections between theatre and the ephemeral, which helps to site the 'loss' of *Common Chorus*, others of his writings restate the enduring power of the classical images, which resides, unhappily, in the fact that they appear repeatedly in the modern news media. Hekabe is the Euripidean character but also all the other old women who punctuate the news with their mourning:

> In my notebooks, where I glue pictures among the drafts of translations from the Greek tragedies I've adapted for the stage, is the recurring image of an old woman appealing to the camera that has captured her agony, or to the heavens that ignore it, in front of a devastated home or before her murdered dead ... . They are in Sarajevo, Kosovo, Grozny, Gaza, Ramallah, Tbilisi, Baghdad, Falluja – women in robes and men in metal helmets as in the Trojan war ... . Hecuba walks out of Euripides from 2,500 years ago straight on to our daily front pages and into our nightly newscasts. To our shame she is news that stays news.[39]

Harrison's introduction addresses this paradox of the persistence of Hekabe, and the disappearance of *Common Chorus II*, by insisting that classics must be reinterpreted for each new occasion and so, implicitly, his current *Trojan Women*, while pertinent, would not be this one.[40] Hekabe is a moment in history rather than a timeless event outside history, but the moment that she represents, in its horror, moves through time and across the world.[41]

Common Chorus II is consigned by Harrison's introduction to a very precise sort of historical oblivion, and it might even be thought poised ready to re-emerge, like Hekabe, into the news, given that power struggles can continue, as we have found after 2001, by many means other than nuclear missiles. On the other hand, historical oblivion may be an appropriate response, because the Cruise missiles that were the play's specific target did in fact leave their leafy Greenham bases, as part of the response to the fall of the Berlin Wall, and there was one Trojan War that did not take place. *Trojan Women*, on the other hand, whether in Greek or in an adaptation, must suppose that the war has happened and could not be stopped. By insistently recalling the Greenham context in many details of the play, moreover, *Common Chorus II* reminds us of other dimensions of that struggle. Not only were the politics of peace at stake, but also the trajectories in theory and practice of feminism. Greenham Common represented certain kinds of feminist experiment with identity and community,[42] and consideration of this aspect might give another perspective on the possible 'fit' between *Trojan Women* and Greenham. The women of Euripides' *Trojan Women* are victims, even if not only victims, whereas the women of Greenham Common by their actions refused that position for themselves and their posterity.[43]

If there is thus not a perfect 'fit' between *Trojan Women* and the context of *Common Chorus II*, that might provoke us to further exploration of the contemporary play's details. For instance, if the women of *Common Chorus II* have, like the Trojan women, been defeated in war, then by whom? On many occasions it seems as if they have been defeated by the soldiers who man the base, who are British like the women, whereas the Americans, who historically were in charge of events, manifest themselves only as disembodied voices and walkie-talkie crackle, to that extent not appearing explicitly as the enemy. At

94

other points, for instance when the women fear being taken over the sea (288-9, 334), or when the Wooden Horse is described as being from the USA (309), the aggressors may be identified as the Americans. Thus the final catastrophe for Troy is announced by 'the headlights of the Cruise convoys' moving towards both the women and the audience (341, 343).[44] The Americans have managed a peaceful invasion of British soil, and both parts of Common Chorus register the subsequent humiliation.[45] Since the Americans were historically meant to be 'allies', the notion of a defeat by them raises the perennial question of the shifting identity of victors and vanquished. This is a point to which we shall return. A perhaps more disturbing possibility canvassed by the play is that we should think of the Americans, in the combination of unseen presence and limitless power, as equivalent to the Greek gods. This would explain Poseidon's American accent (284), and also why the absent Americans seem to be able to hear what is happening on stage (e.g. 303).[46]

There is thus an instability about who the women's victorious enemies are, which is generated in part by the mapping of Greenham realities on to the Greek play's contours, but which also corresponds to the insight of other versions that it is men who are enemies of women. In the Greenham context the antithesis between the prosecution of war and the preservation of life becomes ever more gendered. Other instabilities follow, even in terms of the notion of place, which is central to the Greek play's representation of the women's loss. In Common Chorus II, the women are held as captives, but they are in 'benders', the name for the structures that Greenham women made for themselves.[47] The captive women are not, therefore, in the equivalent of the Greek army's tents. The base, surrounded by barbed wire and defended by the British guards, is presumably the enemy, as it was for the Greenham women; but it also does duty for the Troy that the women are leaving, as when Astyanax falls from the watchtower behind the wire (322). Such blurring of the lines between friend and enemy may be a result of an imperfect mapping of Greenham on to Troy, but in another sense it is a perfect illustration of Kassandra's revelation in the Greek play that victory has become defeat. Troy is both inside and outside the wire because there is no distinction between the victorious and the vanquished, only the mass annihilation characteristic of nuclear combat. The point is made in reference to a sense of place by Lysistrata in *Common Chorus I* (242):

> ... there's no difference between there and here.
> Since Hiroshima what we've done
> Paradoxically's to make the whole Earth one.
> We all look down the barrel of the same cocked gun.

The point is driven home by the women of *Common Chorus II* as they are forced to enact the various implications of Kassandra's paradox.

Not only a sense of place but also a version of history is confounded by various of *Common Chorus II*'s strategies. The play insists several times that all wars should be understood as one. Thus on 311 the anthology of weapons explicitly collapses differences among wars, and uses the iconic image from Vietnam, children 'running on the roads with their flesh in flames', to speak of war in general.[48] The ability to say that all wars are one is what enabled *Trojan Women* to deploy the myth of the Trojan War, as we saw when discussing Sartre, and it is also what enables *Trojan Women* to resurface in its various avatars, including *Common Chorus II*; but it has been criticised for obscuring any more specific politics.[49]

The imperfect mapping of Greenham on to Greece thus has various effects on *Common Chorus II*, and this jostling of Greenham with ancient Greece is not unlike the struggle between myth and contemporary fifth-century realities in Athenian tragedy. Occasionally the specificities of Greenham are carried by the stage directions, which are often long and detailed. For instance, they register that the chorus has its roots in a historical reality when they require that each woman of the chorus bear a name of a historical Greenham woman (289), even though there is no space in the play's dialogue for such naming.

96

Detailed instructions about costume and choreography (295, 297-8) remake Cassandra in the very specific image of a punk, with overtones of the radical lesbian identity often predicated of Greenham women, and align her with the Greenham symbol of the woven web.[50] Other moments are more like that on 307, where the women 'keen' for Troy, in an utterance appropriate both to lamenting ancient Greek women and to those of Greenham, at the same time as brewing up in an inescapably twentieth-century kettle.[51]

Especially thought-provoking is the fact that the sound of the sea, which will take the women of Troy away, is here the sound of the traffic going past the women's camp, or perhaps the sound of the base's generator (287):

> *If ever we hear the sound of the ocean it is the swish of traffic passing Greenham, or the hum of a generator, its throb and rhythm.*

Since the traffic, and the generator, might be features not only of a historical Greenham location but also of other theatrical sites where the play might fetch up, the stage direction takes on a certain metatheatrical quality. Similarly, when Hekabe looks out to sea, it is the same as looking out into the auditorium (287):

> *Hekabe moves closer to the waiting ships in the auditorium, fascinated by them, peering at them, swaying at their motion at anchor.*

These metatheatrical moments collapse the distance between play and spectator as much as between Greenham and Greece.

Metatheatre is a rich source of comedy in *Common Chorus I*, the version of *Lysistrata*, but in *Common Chorus II* the comedy is largely confined to the early scenes with the guards. The guards get a lot of comic mileage out of the inconcinnity between their role as common soldiers and their other roles as Poseidon and Athena (279-84), as in their very first exchange:

Guard 1 (Poseidon):
> From salt, up from deep salt water, up –
> POSEIDON, Poseidon, me. Down there below
> In Europe's bitter waters the NEREIDS...

Guard 2:
> The what?

On 283 Guard 2 also resists his role as Athena: 'I'm not playing a lass, Troy or no Troy'. This metatheatrical self-consciousness responds to *Trojan Women*'s perception that the destruction of the city at least made its name, but the comic dimension legible in the guards' exchanges does not survive the first few scenes.

The opening of the play is significant in another way, in that it takes over from the *Lysistrata* part the counterpoint of male and female voices. In *Common Chorus I* the interplay of male and female voices enacts the overt sexual antagonism that characterises the play and its humour, but in *Common Chorus II* the antagonism obtains between victor and vanquished rather than between two still contending parties. The stage directions make it clear that the counterpoint is also a division (279):

> *[Poseidon] begins to count them [Nereids] off in a military roll-call. As he punches out the names in staccato bursts, female voices pick out the names of the Nereids and make something flowing and female out of them. The two ways of delivery heighten musically the divisions created by the wire.*

Despite the hostility in the roll-call, which is, 'like the obscene taunts and chants of Part One, designed to wake [the women] in the early hours' (279), there is here a possibility of understanding the voices as blending together, which disappears later in the play. There is a brief sharing of 'Here Comes the Bride', cited by both Cassandra (295) and the walkie-talkies (302), but overall the two voices are separated: women's delivery includes keening, singing and dancing, whereas the men are confined to the crackle of walkie-talkies and to 'cruise music' which is a 'counter-music to that of the women' (309). The funeral of Astyanax marks the clearest disjunction between male and female, inside and outside the wire, since the women keen with 'solemn ceremony' whereas the men, the guards, drag the body about with 'hurry and lack of ceremony' (339). A song on the dual nature of fire, which was composed very early on and which does not directly translate any of the Greek text, aligns the fires very clearly with gender (332-3).[52] The sexual antagonism which is thus made into a leading theme of the play, almost as much as it was in *Lysistrata* and *Common Chorus I*, and more than it was in *Trojan Women,* forcibly suggests that the women have been defeated by the men of both sides, by the present British squaddies as well as the absent American supermen. Although this suggestion responds to Kassandra's paradox, it signifies more than the obliteration of differences between victors and defeated; it also offers a verdict on the ways that gender politics intersect with war, mutually reinforcing the sacrifice of women to the distorted priorities of men.

Harrison's stage directions thus stress the gender antagonism that I have suggested is also constitutive of other contemporary versions. In the Greek *Trojan Women*, there simply were not enough men speaking onstage for a counterpoint of voices to emerge. In subsequent adaptations the number of men on stage proliferates, and it is partly perhaps this enlarged number that allows the foregrounding of male brutality towards women. *Trojan Women's* relatively small number of men also means, I suggest, that we cannot very easily objectify and dismiss the male characters on stage. Because they are *not* a horde of violent soldiers, but are the laughable Menelaos and the apparently distressed Talthybios, the events that they set in train perhaps appear all the more terrible, and identification with them, rather than only against them, becomes more readily available.

Since Kassandra's paradox is so vehemently visible in *Common Chorus II*, it is proper to consider the revisions that the figure of the Greek princess and prophetess undergoes in this play. Overall, in *Common Chorus II*, the plot and characters are substantially the same as in the Greek antecedent, so it is in the details that the critical differences between this play and its forebear are legible. The new Cassandra is characterised by very specific sartorial signs from the Britain of the 80s and early 90s such as partly shaved head, green hair, studs and safety pins; she is also decorated with peace badges and a peace banner (295). It is not clear whether the stage directions could envisage a production in which Cassandra was not dressed correspondingly; the aggressively non-feminine aspect of this self-presentation ties it firmly to the Greenham context by aligning it with the 'radical lesbian' trends of some of Greenham's versions of female identity. The punk representation, and the aggression legible within it, is consistent with the obscenity and scatology in Cassandra's speech, and with the overall characterisation of her as 'mad'.

We saw above that there is some dissent over how to understand the madness of Kassandra in the Greek *Trojan Women*, and I suggested that her madness is more staged and ironic than the product of a mind broken under suffering. Here the irony of Cassandra's 'madness' is more pronounced; when she mixes the tune of 'Here Comes the Bride' with the various cheerfully obscene monosyllables of her first song (295-8), drawn from the soldiers' chants in *Common Chorus I*, it is hard to believe that she takes any of it seriously.[53] Even more than in the Greek, this Cassandra's madness, and her mockery of her audiences, paradoxically position her as an authoritative figure. Not only able to induce the queen and chorus to dance with her (297), in a way that is left only as remote possibility in the Greek, she is also able to make a hole in the wire, even though she is prevented from getting through (298). She is the character who is most involved with the Greenham symbols that were in evidence in *Common Chorus I*, providing thus a link between the two plays; she plaits her name into the three peace letters that decorate the wire, making CASSANDRA out of C-N-D (the abbreviation for the Campaign for Nuclear Disarmament), and she is the centre of the Greenham 'web' that the women weave (298-9). On top of this is the authority of her long speech, wherein, as in the Greek, she shows a commanding understanding of the present situation in Troy, its counterpart in Greece, and the whole futility of the war.

Having rehearsed the arguments about victor and vanquished from *Trojan Women*, however, she develops her analysis in a different direction. The Guards are ready to join her in condemnation of Helen, but she *'silences them with a very clear-eyed speech about what happens back home when the troops are away on a ten-year campaign'* (300). What happens, in her speech, is that the wives and children left behind all become sexually corrupt, prostituting themselves or taking lovers in a deadly orgy that combines Lysistratan excess with the despair of *Trojan Women*. The wives in particular have experienced other women, as well as other men, and shudder at the approach of their returning husbands. Any positive heterosexual energy left over from the version of the *Lysistrata* in *Common Chorus I* is thus dissipated by the corrosive ironies of *Common Chorus II*.

This speech, which has no counterpart in *Trojan Women*, also shows elements of the 'unstable mapping' that we have discussed before. Addressing the Guards, Cassandra reminds them that their comrades end up as (301)

A few white dusty ounces
Left in a place the newscaster mispronounces

The 'mispronunciation' makes it very likely that the 'place' at issue is not Troy, but one of the Middle Eastern locations more recently in the news. This 'interference' from the contemporary scene can remind us too that the male aggressors in *Common Chorus II*, whether understood as British or American troops, in the Greenham Common context are not, in fact, suffering, dying, or being deprived of burial at the hands of their loved ones. The telling paradox of Cassandra's vision of war is not, it turns out, fully applicable to her new play, even though it may

represent the truth of nuclear conflict. To thus collapse all wars
into one is, as suggested earlier, both a strength and a weakness
of Harrison's drama.

Two other characters notable for their relations to their
Greek counterparts are Hekabe and Astyanax. Since their
speeches, or lack of them, are close to the Greek, it is again the
stage directions and other 'business' which rewrite these characters. In the case of Hekabe, the new play makes much more
explicit than the Greek the fact that she strives, on so many
occasions, to find something positive to take from the situation.[54] Hekabe, not the chorus, concludes the action with the
words

> Come on, old girl, up. Totter towards the ships,
> and life as a slave. But slavery's still *life*.

In the Greek, Hekabe's last word is indeed 'life', but she is
saying (literally) 'go towards the slavery day of life' so that there
does not seem to be the same emphasis as in Harrison's version.
In earlier scenes the stage directions are quite insistent:

> *There is a sense of blocked hope, futility. It seems that it is
> up to Hekabe, who in some ways has suffered most, once
> more to find the flicker of hope, somewhere.* (317)

> *This [the funeral of Astyanax] is the lowest point for the
> Chorus and once more the responsibility of unearthing even
> the smallest spark of hope is with Hekabe.* (339)

It is the scene prior to the funeral, when Andromache learns of
the sentence against her son, which calls on this quality of
Hekabe's most strongly, and which also displays other striking
differences from the Euripidean handling. Astyanax is intro-
duced after the choral song, and he is wearing a brightly col-
oured anorak and scarf that distinguish him from the women of
Troy. Hekabe and Andromache engage in their familiar dialogue, but it is slightly altered when '*The bleakness of An-*

dromache makes Hekabe take Astyanax to her, as if to prevent the hope he represents being blasted by his mother's despair' (315). As Andromache continues her lament for Hector, and comparison of herself with the dead Polyxena, Hekabe *'covers his ears so he doesn't hear his mother's black despair. She rocks his head to and fro, humming the "swaysong" from before'* (316). Then, as Hekabe follows the imperative to 'find the flicker of hope', she takes Astyanax *'nearer the ships to look at them as if they were something exciting for the boy'*. Her words about the sailors on ships, and how they cope with storms, are now directed towards him as well as towards his mother, and she adopts a cheerful, coaxing tone to explain ships to him. Astyanax responds by going forward in order to see the ships better, leaving his grandmother to finish her conversation with his mother in a bleaker register (317). Implied, then, is the conclusion that Astyanax understands a lot of what is going on around him, even though the scene makes more of his childish status than do other versions. Hekabe's taking thought for his understanding is particularly wrenching in the context of Talthybius' errand. Although, as in the Greek, Astyanax has no lines of his own, he is said to understand what is happening to him when Talthybius announces his death (320), which it is not clear he does in the Greek. In both plays, however, he cries and clings to his mother. Nor does this version shrink, as some versions do, from having Andromache invite the Greeks to 'eat him' (321). This version thus explores the full horror of the child's death, increasing the pathos by elaborating in naturalistic style on the issue of his understanding.

Although space does not permit a full account of Harrison's language in this play, we can note that along with the 'interference' between Greece and Greenham comes a vertiginous swooping among registers of discourse, which is also characteristic of Euripidean drama. Obscenities and very colloquial registers are combined with relatively unmarked, ordinary speech, and certain episodes are underlined by rhyme and music. The choral songs display tremendous anger at the gods which, like the anger of the guards against the women, is marked by liberal obscenity (e.g. 333). The final meeting of Hekabe and Astyanax combines registers in a powerful way. Hekabe describes herself and Hector as 'granny' and 'Daddy' throughout this scene (337, 338), but the 'epitaph' that she pronounces for the child is 'poetic' in the sense of displaying both an archaic word, 'herein', and inversion in the word order:

> A little child is herein laid
> Killed by the Greeks who were afraid.

The funeral is the 'lowest point' (339), but Harrison's version ends by affirming 'life' (343, the last word of the play), in the face of threatened annihilation, exactly as the historical Greenham women did.[55]

Brendan Kennelly, *The Trojan Women*

Kennelly's version, first produced and published in 1993, is more of a translation than a full-scale adaptation like that of Harrison, but it makes some intriguing choices about how to render the play. Some critics have suggested that it is legibly Irish, and concerned with Irish conditions, but others have suggested that if it is to be understood as commenting on the state of Ireland, this may be less in specific historical reference than in the overall representation of oppression, particularly by the male.[56] There is also, especially towards the end, an interrogation of history in terms of the perniciousness of memory and the necessity of forgetting (207).[57] While no Greek gods are involved, 'God' is frequently invoked, which again may be thought to speak to Irish experience. As with other recent versions of *Trojan Women*, the identification of victors and victims with male and female is a prominent theme, and the play can even be characterised as anti-male rather than anti-war.[58]

Most critics have found it hard to ignore what Kennelly himself says about the play's genesis and focus:

3. Twentieth-century Receptions

Almost fifty years ago, I heard women in the village where I grew up say of another woman, 'She's a Trojan woman, God bless her', meaning she had tremendous powers of endurance and survival, was determined to overcome different forms of disappointment and distress, was dogged but never insensitive, obstinate but never black-scowling, and seemed eternally capable of renewing herself ... I wasn't writing a hymn to heroic women although I believe a man might spend his lifetime praising certain women and count that life well spent.[59]

Consonant with this statement is that by Poseidon, as he opens the play, when he claims that 'women will rule the world' (141). Even though it is a god that speaks, the statement invites scrutiny. If divine, it ought to be true, and yet 2,500 years after the dramatic date of the utterance, it is manifestly not; on the other hand, the god is by his own account (141) old and tired and in need of good dreams, so this statement may be part of his senile meanderings. Alternatively, we are free to understand the statement as one about the future that is uttered in the actual present, not at the dramatic date of the fall of Troy, so that the time of women's rule is yet to come. In either case the utterance is vulnerable to the criticism that feminist politics wish to redefine the meanings of 'rule' rather than simply switch places between men and women.[60] Altogether it is not obvious how far we can trust Poseidon's words.

This reservation is relevant because Poseidon mobilises many of the concerns that will prove to be among the drama's more important. Like the women later, he is convinced that men go to war because they love to kill, rather than for any more elevated reasons (143). In particular, war is far more sexualised here than in any other version,[61] so that it is driven by the lusts of men more than even by their anger or fear (143):

The old style is with us still:
Kill and love! Love and kill!

105

Connected to this insight is the play's emphasis on rape, which as an organised means of subjection and revenge has taken on a new prominence in contemporary warfare.[62] Even Hecuba envisages her future in terms of sexual slavery in a way that was never canvassed for the Euripidean queen (147). Surprisingly, though, it is precisely this aspect of her future that Hecuba identifies as a form of freedom, especially in her resounding closing speech (210):[63]

> What does it matter if I fuck
> Some tricky itchy stinking weasel of a Greek
> So long as I know what I'm doing
> And why I'm doing it?
> And when he's fucking me
> May I not smile
> And ask the very face of darkness –
> Darling, who is free?

Against the lust and violence of men, Poseidon in his opening speech poses the spirit of women, particularly that of Hecuba, and in this he is in agreement with the preface (143):

> But was there ever such a spirit in a woman's body?
> Hecuba will fight to the end
> And beyond the end.

Since this account of Hecuba is repeated elsewhere in the play (147, 150, 204), there is little sense that Hecuba is also struggling with what attitude to take to her predicament; she does not veer back and forth between believing in the gods and dismissing them, as did the Euripidean Hekabe. Even when she reprises Greek Hekabe's moment of complete disillusionment with the gods, after the death of Astyanax, she manages to extract some affirmation from the situation. Greek Hekabe notes that at least the Trojans will be remembered in songs. Kennelly's Hecuba finds what she sees as a truth about herself and humanity, not just poetry (202):

And then amid the dust, amid the wrong,
amid the trembling hills and cities
amid the streets of rubble and the fields of death
I heard the music of our hearts
I knew the everlasting beauty of the song
Of earth and heaven.
I kissed God's hand! I am real. I am so real
I am not afraid to look into the eyes of God.

Even as it pits the women against an enemy that consists of the whole other half of humankind, then, the play is more affirming than any of its predecessors. To achieve this affirmation, however, the play declines to engage overtly with power politics and instead, sends the women inside, to their inner spiritual selves, there to gain strength. Hence, again, Hecuba's closing speech, but also that of Andromache, especially 173, where she goes well beyond the Greek in terms of self-awareness:

And yet I clearly see
That if my body is a slave
An untouched portion of my mind is free.

To find another kind of freedom from the one they have lost is, we may conclude, the source of strength of Kennelly's strong women. In this the Trojan women all, paradoxically, learn from Cassandra, who goes down into herself to find her 'special light' (157 – also Andromache's term on 173).[64] Along with the emphasis on inner strength goes a focus on how the women will learn from their conquerors. In this respect the new version plays an interesting variation on 'Kassandra's paradox' of the inferiority of the victor and the superiority of the vanquished. In the Harrison, the point was that the two became interchangeable in the crucible of nuclear war. In the Kennelly, the 'women will rule' because they have the inner spirit not only to resist their conquerors but also to learn from them. What they learn is, occasionally at least, how to be 'winners' instead of 'losers'. Several of the Trojan women speak of themselves in this way, and Talthybius agrees (151, 161, 174). At 196 Hecuba is quite explicit – 'Learn from your oppressor!' With this stance, in another ugly paradox, the women are themselves learning from Helen.

The Helen scene, as so often in other versions, not least the Greek, upsets any previous emotional and philosophical calculations. Here the notion that women will rule, and the celebration of women's strength, comes up against the nature of Helen's domination. Indeed the working definition of women as the ones who suffer also runs up against Helen's determination to do no such thing, and to evade suffering simply by means of her identity as a female. This is why the scene turns on the definition of female, as when Helen asks Hecuba repeatedly 'What do you see?' and Hecuba answers repeatedly 'A cunt' (192-3). When Helen herself speaks, however, she delivers a developed philosophical meditation that sweeps all before it (184-8). More even than the Greek Helen, she brings out the absurdity of the quest for the guilty subject in a context where it is men who long, erotically, to go to war, and where this root cause must be correspondingly disguised (185):

> There must always be someone to blame, Menelaus.
> At home men and women blame me for their dead,
> for all the young men lost in this long war.
> Why do they go to war?
> They go to war to fuck each other to death
> ...
> Tens of thousands play war's murderous game
> and when the game is over
> and the dead must be buried
> ...
> someone must be blamed
> for what had to happen.

The scene degenerates into an attempted lynching like that of Serban, with the women howling sexual insults (193-4). This formal innovation sets the scene apart from the rest of the play, pointing up its centrality, even though the scene undermines the ostensible theme of the rest of the drama.

Charles Mee, *The Trojan Women 2.0: a love story*

The Trojan Women 2.0: a love story is part of Charles Mee's remaking project, which he describes thus:[65]

There is no such thing as an original play.

None of the classical Greek plays were original: they were all based on earlier plays or poems or myths ... Whether we mean to or not, the work we do is both received and created, both an adaptation and an original, at the same time. We re-make things as we go.

The plays on this website were mostly composed in the way that Max Ernst made his Fatagaga pieces toward the end of World War I: texts have often been taken from, or inspired by, other texts. Among the sources for these pieces are the classical plays of Euripides as well as texts from the contemporary world.

I think of these appropriated texts as historical documents – as evidence of who and how we are and what we do.

He describes the remaking of *Trojan Women* in more detail thus: 'I have pillaged the structures and contents of the plays of Euripides and Berlioz and stuff out of Soap Opera Digest and the evening news and the internet';[66] 'incorporating shards of our contemporary world, to lie, as in a bed of ruins, within the frame of the classical world. It incorporates, also, texts by the survivors of Hiroshima and of the Holocaust, by Slavenka Drakulic, Zlatko Dizdarevic, Georges Bataille, Sei Shonagon, Elaine Scarry, Hannah Arendt, the Kama Sutra, Amy Vanderbilt, and the Geraldo show.'[67] Audiences have responded enthusiastically to Mee's pastiches, and directors also relish the opportunities to remake their own plays out of his shards, as Mee actively invites them to. His playscript sometimes leaves directorial decisions wide open (64, 76), and in the matter of the music that is an integral part of his productions, other directors quite often use completely different songs from the ones suggested in the playscript published on the web.[68]

The Euripidean-derived part of the 'remake' is set, predictably, in the aftermath of a city's downfall, where its men have been killed and its raped women wait for allotment as slaves. The 'Greek' elements of the play jar energetically with directions such as that the women are 'dark-skinned "3rd-world" women making computer components at little work tables' (1), and that the members of the Trojan royal family wear 'silk Yves St Laurent that has been torn' (2). If we conclude from this opening that the play will make links among war, sexual exploitation of women, and economic exploitation of the Third World, however, we shall be mistaken, because the play proceeds to dilate mainly on the brutality of men, and male warfare, to women. The royal women and the named, individuated, and indeed opinionated chorus women offer a catalogue of contemporary horrors from the Holocaust and Hiroshima, with some more passing reference to the more contemporary struggle in the former Yugoslavia.

The figure of Hecuba has changed from the Greek in significant ways. She is still a maternal figure who wishes to manage the pain of her country women and who sees her task as the maintenance of some civilised standards (3, 28), but she repudiates revenge until the last moment. As in Berlioz, the women are aware that Aeneas is still alive, and the chorus women long for him to take revenge on the Greeks. But Hecuba says (6):

Let it end ...
Then let it end here.
Let it end now.
What ever could make you want to start again?

Later on in the scene with Helen the chorus will again urge revenge, and Hecuba, unlike her Greek self, will stop them (39).

As with the Harrison, there are more men in this version than in the Greek. Talthybius is accompanied by two Special Forces soldiers, Bill and Ray Bob, who provide almost choral, and almost comic, commentaries on the situation: 'This is how men are' (7, 10). When they recount atrocities they are calm and philosophical: 'I don't say I like it this way ... I can live with it' (8). Meanwhile Talthybius, with similar obtuseness, combines his orders to the women with meditation on the possibilities that persist in the aftermath of war (11):

> No sugar for the after dinner coffee, to be sure,
> And the cost of a filet of sole is atrocious –
> Yet one can believe
> A good life is still possible in the world
> It may be that there are throat germs everywhere
> But one can still attend a concert
> Or hear a reading of Claudel's poetry

The new play keeps the pattern of encounters with the 'daughters of Hekabe' that the Greek play offered, but gives greater pungency in each case to the sexual content. Thus with Andromache, the play takes the Greek character's account of her life as a 'good woman' and remakes it to the limit and beyond; in shock (12), Andromache recounts endless trivial details of her past life, but becomes more and more obsessive, mingling recitation of the rules of etiquette with grief for sexual opportunities that she would have taken had she known it was all going to end so soon (16-17). As the chorus women disagree among themselves over how much pity to extend to the fallen princess, they start to vie with each other in exchanging stories of domestic violence, suffered and inflicted, with Bill and Ray Bob. When this exchange concludes with a long lecture from one choruswoman, presumably ironic, on 'feminist utopias', Talthybius suddenly notices the 'dead doll' (12) that Andromache carries and seizes it as 'A living heir to the throne' (23). Despite the unforgettable treatments in earlier plays, and despite this play's intriguing equivocation between life and death, however, the scene is not prolonged, because Cassandra rushes in, not with a paradoxical account of victory and defeat but with vindictive rage, shared by the chorus, for sexual violence against men, which fuels her plan to murder Agamemnon.

The 'daughters of Hekabe' for this play turn out to include Polyxena, who occupies the next scene and imports Euripides' *Hekabe* into this version of *Trojan Women*. Polyxena is sentenced to be sacrificed to Achilles, as in the Greek *Hekabe*, and as there, she accepts her death, but not with a heroic speech about avoiding slavery. Instead, as befits a teenager, she discourses naively about fate, destiny and numerology, and wishes she could have lived a little longer if only to get the answer to pressing questions such as (30):

> Why do guys drink out of the milk carton?
> And how come they like to play air guitar?
> Why is a guy who sleeps around a stud
> but a girl who does is a slut?

Bill and Ray Bob solemnly try to provide answers.

After Polyxena's exit to death, Menelaus enters, soon followed by Helen. To judge from reviews, this sleazy couple often grabs audience attention more effectively than the wronged women, and their duets can be the high point of a production.[69] Without the sophistic complexity of the Greek, this Helen is explicitly described as 'the seductive survivor, the master of "feminine wiles" (not used by any of the other women in the play)' (36). She runs briskly through the arguments made by Euripides' Helen, and deals decisively with the interruptions from the chorus calling for her punishment and death, while Hecuba, as we have seen, takes up the unexpected position of opposing these calls. As Helen and Menelaus leave together, united, Helen rounds on Hecuba and the chorus, dispelling any vestige of ambiguity in her character by her words (40):

And you,
you worthless pieces of shit
don't give me any of your fucking attitude
try to cut me down
with your whining
...
You use a fucking dildo,
You fucking
Losers

The 'dead doll' that Andromache carried is not seen again, and instead, it is Polyxena's body that is brought back for Hecuba to prepare. As the chorus narrate her heroic death from Euripides' *Hekabe*, the Hecuba of this play finally yearns for revenge, and in this play, unlike in Euripides' *Trojan Women*, she can get it. Aeneas is also brought in to her, and although he is trembling, unmanned by fear and by what he has seen, she charges him (45):

Your time has come
To find all those who have survived,
Take them to a new country
Build a home.
Make it strong.
Put your trust in power alone.
Make a nation that can endure.
And when you have,
Come back,
Reduce these Greeks and their world
To ruins.
Destroy their cities.
Burn them.
Pull down their homes.
Leave them wounded and alone
Abandoned.
Let them bleed to death on their own graves.

All this, of course, we know comes to pass. Hecuba has been forced by the pressure of events into the position that she repudiated, and identified with men, at the outset: (9)

Why is it at the end of war
The victors can imagine nothing better
Than to remake the conditions
That are the cause of war?

She is thus more like Hekabe of *Hekabe* than of *Trojan Women*, and more so, because her revenge is on a world-historical scale.

The second half of the remake is set in Carthage, ruled by the black queen Dido, and reimagined as a sensuous paradise full of athletic women who alternately exercise and relax in a luxurious spa. Set designers have a ball with this part.[70] The all-female environment, where the chorus women sing of love, is interrupted by Aeneas and veterans from the Trojan War, men who have been defeated and who talk in very different ways from Bill and Ray Bob (although they can of course be played by the same actors) about their love of women, and even their desire to wear women's clothes and be women (51). When Dido enters, she immediately begins to undress Aeneas and bathe with him in a hot tub (53), while the chorus women discourse to the veterans of sexual positions and pleasures that they know (54). The men respond with narration of some of the events that have traumatised them (56-7), and this counterpoint between masculine and feminine versions of the world persists throughout the play, but in a much less threatening vein than in the first part. This counterpoint does not exempt either women or men from the pains of love, however, and the play takes Dido and Aeneas through a gamut of emotions that are only partly articulated by the torch songs and jazz standards that they sing. Dido reads the Tarot cards, in a scene that is mischievously self-conscious about the possibilities of building narratives from random encounters (60-1), but comes up against the movement of destiny that necessarily accompanies anyone called 'Aeneas'. He begins to talk of the 'promises' that

114

he has made (70), and the quarrel that ensues also moves to a world-historical scale with its coordination of male and female, white and black, identity and difference, realism and optimism (73-4). The chorus women and veterans join in, and the quarrel ends with Dido drowning Aeneas in the hot tub – or not (76):

> [While the chorus sings this final song,
> Aeneas drags himself from the hot tub.
> He is nearly dead –
> or else, he doesn't drag himself from the tub,
> and he is dead.]

The stage directions further indicate that Dido and Aeneas, and all the men and women, eventually find their way back to each other, and although the play does not explicitly say this, we may well conclude that in this version Aeneas does not leave, either because he is dead or because he is in love, so Rome does not get founded and the Trojan women do not, in fact, avenge their dead. While few responses to the play treat it as philosophically ambitious,[71] we can discern here an engaged meditation on the power of the remaking to overcome violence, or perhaps instead to instigate its own.

Ellen McLaughlin, *The Trojan Women*, and Karen Hartman, *Troy Women*

The Trojan Women 2.0: a love story was produced several times around the turn of the century, when the new forms that violence took, in the former Yugoslavia and in Iraq, were beginning to exert pressure on politics and literature alike. Several other versions were produced around the world as part of responses to the new international situation, and unlike the versions discussed so far, they were often produced by women. In 1995 Annie Castledine directed *Women of Troy* at the National Theatre, London, which attracted critical attention partly because its Greeks were costumed and spoke as Americans. A production directed by Debbie Challis at the University of Birmingham in 1996 was dedicated to the women of Bosnia, Rwanda, Iraq and Afghanistan, and Jane Montgomery's acclaimed production in Cambridge in 1998 set the play explicitly in the Balkans. The 1999 production by Joanne Akalaitis, in Washington, did not so clearly reference contemporary conflicts, but its set invoked the ovens of the Holocaust, and it opened with a scene of women being forcibly shaved, like concentration camp inmates, and raped. Critical accounts suggest that audiences would necessarily have been reminded of more recent conflicts, in the former Yugoslavia, as well as those of the mid-century.[72] They also read an indictment of American policy in the way that Astyanax was held aloft by Greek soldiers in an apparent parody of the iconic Iwo Jima flag-raising.[73] In the early part of this century, productions professional and amateur have often been set in Muslim cultures, and in 2004 a production in Australia gave rise to an unscheduled audience discussion of the war in Iraq.[74] Katie Mitchell's production in London in 2007 was not explicitly set in the Middle East, but all the critical discussion of the production understood that the Iraq war was an inescapable context. The production, which Mitchell had described as her attempt to 'understand' conflict in the Middle East,[75] was set in a grim warehouse where the women were held, with chorus women in evening gowns, which made them look as if they had been snatched away from a party, and in which they occasionally performed ballroom dances together. While such dancing is a Mitchell trademark, we can see that it also connects this production to the work of Mee. The production was criticised, and praised, for cutting the Greek text by almost half, including the roles of the deities, and by rendering Cassandra so demented as to be incomprehensible to the audience.[76]

The version by Ellen McLaughlin was first staged in 1996 in New York, and its production was an event of theatrical importance because it was acted entirely by amateurs who were refugees from the former Yugoslavia. While the women involved came from different sides in the contemporary conflict, the roles of Helen and Menelaos were cut from the translation so that no actor would have to play the 'enemy'. McLaughlin's description of the process of production is a homage to the actors as well as an acknowledgement of the power of the play.[77]

Extraordinarily demanding on the actors, the play was often delivered simultaneously in English, Serbo-Croatian and Albanian, and the roles were typically shared among two or more participants. Emotionally too, of course, the production was more than usually draining on its participants, themselves refugees from lost cities. In 2003 a slightly different version, which restored Helen, was produced and subsequently published in 2005, and this published version was produced again in 2008 in California to great critical acclaim. Although the production eschewed direct reference to America's wars in the Middle East, apart from being costumed in modern dress, reviewers nonetheless made firm connections to Iraq.[78] Since McLaughlin's work had already included several adaptations of Greek tragedy, including a *Persians* which was avowedly written as 'a direct response to the American invasion of Iraq in March 2003' (254), such connections were readily available.

The published adaptation again requires careful work from the chorus, the members of which split the lines among themselves, 'dovetailing and overlapping' (91). Incorporating the reminiscences of the Yugoslavian women who were the first chorus in 1996 (e.g. 91-3), the choral songs often diverge considerably from the Greek, and they offer a series of lyrical meditations on the beauties of Troy (e.g. 118). The moral calculus of this version is also different from the Greek, and not only because there is no Athena to plot the destruction of the victors, and no mention by Cassandra or Talthybius of the difficulties awaiting the homecoming conquerors. Although Hecuba is at first clear about her role – ' It will be for me to make order out of this chaos' (93) – she later shifts positions. The role of Helen is made more central, so that she appears on stage three times, while the scenes with Cassandra, Andromache and the baby Astyanax are correspondingly shorter than in the Greek. Helen's role is also more overtly sympathetic. In her early appearance, just after Poseidon and while the Trojan women

117

are still sleeping on the ground, Helen seems to mourn for Troy. Entering again after Cassandra and before Andromache, she engages in a long and complex debate with Hecuba, which works several twists on the Greek. Since gods are not invoked, the women do not argue about them, so Hecuba indicts Helen for her various mythical acts of selfish gratification, while Helen responds by repeatedly rewriting her myth to redefine that very self. As in the Greek, she comes with a message that is hard to hear. Addressing Hecuba and the chorus women, she draws a new parallel between herself and them; she has endured for years the subjection and degradation that they are about to experience (102):

HELEN
Slavery is new to you. No wonder you chafe at it. When you've endured it as long as I have, years and years, you'll learn to stand up to it without so much self-pity.
And then you'll know what I have had to bear.
HECUBA
What have you ever borne besides a lover's weight?
HELEN
The contempt of the world.
You'll know soon enough. When you rise from your raping beds, wiping your eyes and smoothing your skirts down over your thighs, now purple with your new masters' handprints, perhaps you'll think of me. When you run from your conquerors and find no mercy anywhere, only veiled eyes, turned heads and snickering; when servants, children and strangers on the street spit at you and call you a whore, then, then, oh, I hope you think of me.

Hecuba is unmoved by this, as perhaps we should be, and since there is no Menelaos in this version to exact punishment, threatens Helen herself (102-3):

HECUBA
We may be slaves, but we still have the freedom to take

118

our justice as we find it. What can keep us from having our revenge now that you are finally helpless against our hatred and without protection?
HELEN
When have I ever had protection?
This is so familiar.
And hatred?
It's all I've ever known.

In the absence of Menelaos as judge, Hecuba, who in this incarnation has perhaps embraced her moral degradation more than in others, passes sentence: 'Let beauty perish with everything else./Take her and defile her' (105). In a scene reminiscent of the Serban and the Kennelly, the chorus women drag her off, then bring her back with her hair shorn, her face bloodied and her arms tied to a yoke. She defies them (107):

The girl you could have punished died long ago.
I became the Helen. The eating flame of beauty.
She happened to the world.
It had nothing to do with me.

Since Andromache and Astyanax enter after Helen's final exit, her terrible self-knowledge perhaps overshadows even their scenes.

Hecuba is hard with her other 'daughter' Andromache, too. In another inversion of the Greek, Andromache endeavours to find a way to cope with her new life with Neoptolemos, rather than envying the dead: 'Perhaps there will be some light left for me in this life, not just the watery dim light of duty and memory. Perhaps I will forget' (108). Unlike her Greek self, Hecuba sentences Andromache to continue to honour Hektor's memory and live 'in gratitude and service to his memory ... Without joy ... without hope' (109). Even she, however, imagines the hope embodied in Astyanax, which is of course felled by the entrance of Talthybios. Talthybios is a sympathetic figure, who assures Andromache (and us?) that 'He will not know ...

He will not understand' (112) but who exits with the baby in silence without the last speech about not being the man for the job. He re-enters almost immediately with the corpse, but there is only a short funeral speech over Astyanax because he insists 'To the ships. It is over' (116). Hecuba and the choruswomen exit to the words 'We must go' rather than with any affirmation of 'life'.

The adaptation by Karen Hartman, first produced in 1997 but published in 2005, follows the Greek more closely in that it retains all the characters and the scenes.[79] In other respects, however, it diverges, especially in the treatment of the chorus, which is here individuated into five separate women: 1 an attendant to Hecuba, 2 her daughter who is still a girl, 3 'Spirited', 4 'Romantic' and 5 'Mother of sons'. The first chorus woman especially retains respectful forms of address to Hecuba, which jar very effectively in Hecuba's changed context, while the second steals the scene at moments such as when she practises jumping off a rock – like Astyanax (60). Cassandra is rewritten to appear completely sane, if inappropriately knowing, with a delicious line in scorching irony:

> I always get so sentimental at these events.
> Thank Hymen for a torch to dry my tears.
> Let's all share happy memories of the bride.
> Let's have a women's ritual.
> ...
> Maybe have a little talk with me Mother about whisper?
> Because I'm kind of starting to blush
> Just thinking
> about loving
> Such a big, big, hero.
> ...
> What if I gag
> or scream in a way he finds unappealing?
> What if I bleed too much
> Or not enough?
> What if I fart?

She taunts Talthybius, the herald whom she nicknames
Harold, even more fiercely than her Greek counterpart, and
exits completely confident with her starring role in Agamemnon's future.[80]

Subsequent scenes with the other 'daughters of Hekabe',
Andromache and Helen, are not compellingly different from the
Greek, and Astyanax, as in the Greek, is a child rather than a
baby. The choral songs, however, offer significant variations.
One explores, in conjunction with the 'Voice of the City', the
possibility that Troy is to blame at some level for her own
destruction: 'We must be willing to get historical ... We must
confront the painful possible that we the people now women of
Troy have had a hand' (48). Another plays with the name and
fate of Helen obsessively, rhyming she, me, and sea until it
concludes in words that seem to confuse the distance between
Helen and her accusers (60):[81]

> Helen breaks and eats and trades my Troy
> Burns and maims my Troy
> Flame take her sea break her remake her as me.
> 4: Mother to be.
> 5: Unwilling to flee.
> 3: Nothing like she.

At the end of the play too the chorus has a special role, for they
begin to speak as if from a different future that imagines the
persistence of Troy as the 'second cradle'. The pseudo-academic
distance then dissolves into fragments (66-7):

> 3: What were we called?
> 4: Where were the crops?
> 5: Which linguistic system did this civilization use?
> 1: Why are the unearthed bodies disproportionately male?
> ...
> 3: Evidence points to contemporeality with the Greek.
> Harmonimity. Civilus. Ethic and art.
> 4: Troy: A Multi-Millennial Perspective. We ask our

pointed question – what would be the West with a second cradle?
5: New scholarship emphasizes perfect gender in ancient
3: strength and warmth
4: an idyllic
...
1: Which war?

Almost all the women exit before the play's final moment, which is shared between choruswoman 2, the young girl, who picks up some of Troy's dust, and Hecuba, who is already becoming a dog.

Femi Osofisan, *The Women of Owu*

The Women of Owu was first staged at the Chipping Norton Theatre in 2004, to considerable critical acclaim, and produced at least once more before being published, in slightly altered form, in 2006.[82] Responding to Sartre as well as to Euripides, it springs further surprises both of content and of form. Osofisan's dramaturgy is distinguished by the twists and turns, and what Gibbs calls 'ambushes' that are laid on for the unsuspecting audience or reader.[83] While this technique is always immensely effective, it is perhaps especially so if an audience 'knows' what to expect from exposure to an antecedent.[84] To this end, Osofisan's dramas have engaged with the Nigerian writers Wole Soyinka and J.P. Clark, as well as with Sophocles, Anouilh, Gogol and Feydeau. The adaptation of *Trojan Women* here both effects changes to the play and meditates on the nature of change itself.

'A Note on the Play's Genesis' (vii) explicitly ties the play to the period of its first production, 'in the season of the Iraqi war'.[85] Osofisan represents himself as 'pondering' over the adaptation of Euripides while remembering the 'tragic Owu'. Such memories were fostered because the Yoruba city Owu had lasted out a seven-year siege by the 'Allied Forces' of Ijebu and Ife, at the conclusion of which the males were executed and the women enslaved. 'The Allied Forces had attacked [Owu] with the pretext of liberating the flourishing market of Apomu from Owu's control' (vii). Since the Ijebu and Ife troops probably did not call themselves 'the Allied Forces', this is likely to be read as an invocation of the contemporary British and American escapade in Iraq. When we read that the Forces used the 'pretext of liberating', we are almost certain we are in the late twentieth and early twenty-first century, but the 'flourishing market' is explicit about the economic motives that in the historical Iraqi context were usually muted by official discourse. This apparent candour about motive, however, will be massively complicated later on in the play.

Whereas *Trojan Women* opens with a deity who explains the context and introduces the characters, the ancestral deity Anlugbua, who opens *Women of Owu,* has no idea at all about the siege and the defeat, and has to be filled in by the two women he meets.[86] The women display a sharp political awareness, commenting on their defeat that (8):

Nowadays,
When the strong fight the weak, it's called
A Liberation War
To free the weak from oppression.
Nowadays, in the new world order, it is suicide to be weak.

The god concludes: 'It is the law of victory, the law/of defeat' (7), but when he first finds out about the city's fate, he cannot understand why his people did not call on him, as he had told them to (3). Conversely, the women, once they have gotten over their fright at seeing the god, can't understand why he didn't help them earlier (7). The scene is one of mutual incomprehension, and it ends with the parties further apart; Anlugbua departs lamenting his lack of worshippers, and the women leave with stinging rebukes for the gods' lack of concern (9). So far, so Euripidean; the god even admits that he is 'shamed' (9) by the women, which is a conclusion often invited by Euripidean gods even if never articulated. But we should also note that gods and humans both claim to have done the correct thing – offered help, or asked for help – and to have received no answering gesture from the other side. Which party to the disagreement should we believe? As the play unfolds, the women of Owu will become increasingly complex figures, and the play will make it very hard to judge among competing claims to moral stature.

The following scene introduces the old woman sprawling on the ground, the Hekabe-figure, Erelu Afin, who like Hekabe shares the scene with the chorus leader and women of the chorus. In his analysis of the play, Budelmann notes that 'communality' is a central issue, both in terms of very skilful writing for the chorus and because the community of women gathered on-stage is itself an object of scrutiny.[87] Although they support and elaborate the action with song and dance, in normal choral fashion, they also often speak lines separately, and do not always relate harmoniously to one another, but quarrel (e.g. 17). The chorus leader operates as a separate source of authority, usually in collaboration with Erelu Afin but occasionally, particularly towards the end of the play, with a more complex relationship (62-3).

Not only are the internal relations of the chorus different from those in the Greek, but their attitude to what is happening to them offers many contrasts. Here they begin with abject lamentation, but move to anger and a storm of curses against their conquerors that is completely absent from the Greek. Later on (38) their curses will culminate in baring their breasts, which in Yoruba culture is a very threatening gesture, fraught with danger for the onlooker. Like the women of the first scene, the chorus in the second see through the pretensions of the victors with a blast of sarcasm (12-13):

> Erelu: Savages! You claim to be more civilized than us
> But did you have to carry out all this killing and carnage
> To show you are stronger than us? Did you
> Have to plunge all these women here into mourning
> Just to seize control over our famous Apomu market
> Known all over for its uncommon merchandise?

Woman: No, Erelu, what are you saying, or
　Are you forgetting?
　They do not want our market at all –
Woman: They are not interested in such petty things
　As profit –
Woman: Only in lofty, lofty ideas, like freedom:
Woman: Or human rights …

Contemporary terms like 'human rights' again invite a comparison with the Euro-American invasions of Iraq, which were repeatedly accused of disguising economic motives with talk of noble political ideals. Endowed by suffering with a moral intelligence that enables them to see through these politics, the women of Owu can play ironically with the categories of 'savage' and 'civilised'.[88] What is signally different from the Greek antecedent, however, is that Owu, Ijebu and Ife are all Yoruba, so that a crucial identity obtains between the aggressors and victims, the victors and vanquished, even before the levelling effect of war gets under way.

Other potential differences are similarly eroded. Since the play is set in what becomes Nigeria, we might expect the war to unfold between colonisers and colonised – this would also resonate with the oblique references to the Middle East. However, when the white man is invoked, he does not play a role particularly different from that of the African. Thus, when the women prepare themselves mentally for existence as slaves (17), the slave-owners will include other Yoruba as well as the white men who supplied the guns to the Allied Forces in the first place (8, 16-17). Responding, perhaps, to these clues, as well as to the news that the ancestor Anlugbua has deserted Owu, the chorus leader concludes that 'The lesson is clear. It's us, not the gods,/who create war. It's us, we human beings, who can kill it' (15). This 'lesson', that human fates are in human hands, will be emphasised at other points in the play. Its opposite is also articulated in several encounters, as when Erelu Afin, unable to comfort her women, explains: 'In defeat, dear women, always expect the worst./That is the law of combat. The law of defeat'

(16). The status of this 'law' of helplessness, and its relation to the 'lesson' of agency, will become increasingly complex.

In *Trojan Women*, Athena joins Poseidon at the beginning to plan the shipwreck of the Greeks, but here, Anlugbua does not meet his female counterpart until after the scene between Erelu and the chorus. Anlugbua is joined by Lawumi, his ancestor, who like Athena, is responsible for the destruction of the city. The striking difference is that here, destruction is a punishment not for the wrong vote in a beauty contest, but for the city's own prior act of desecration (19):

> Owu forgot its history, forgot its origins!
> Your people became drunk with prosperity!
> And in their giddiness, they dared to send their army
> Against Ife! Imagine it!
> They razed the town down and reduced it to dust!

While we are recovering from this revelation about the city of the helpless suffering women on stage before us, Anlugbua counters (19):

> But are you forgetting, mother? It was
> The Ifes who first attacked Owu, at
> The market of Apomu –

Thankfully, we think, we can now have our 'victims' restored to us – but we can't, because Lawumi continues (19):

> Because the Owus were selling
> Other Yoruba into slavery! ...
> The only way to stop them was by force!

Since Anlugbua has no retort to this statement, we must, for the purposes of the play, accept it; the people of Owu were the initial aggressors, and they were enslaving other Yoruba rather than, for instance, stealing wives (about which peccadillo Herodotos 1.1-4 is highly dismissive). While the Greek *Trojan Women* can be read as suspicious of the attempt to find a cause of the Trojan War, this play has a different approach; the search for the object of blame will not be futile, because it will find out the guilty, but the guilty will be those we least thought possible, the very Owu who are the objects of our compassion.[89] *Trojan Women* hinted at the culpability of the Trojans, but declined to serve up as complete an indictment as this. Our vision of the Owu women must split, so that we pity their suffering while being aware of the suffering they inflicted on others. As slavers, can they retain the high ground that was theirs when they perceived the moral bankruptcy of their opponents?[90]

Lawumi's plans, like those of Athena, now involve the destruction of the 'Greeks', here the Ijebu and men of Ife. Since they defiled her temple with the corpses of suppliants, they must suffer on their homeward journey: 'Human beings, it is clear, learn/Only from suffering and pain' (21). Audiences have critiqued the goddess for her caprice and pettiness, but since the most savage story she has told us is of the humans' behaviour, not the gods', we might conclude instead that she is an incurable optimist for believing that humans can learn at all.

The guilt of the Owu, as narrated by Lawumi, marks a distance from the moral calculus of *Trojan Women*, alters the relation between gods and humans from what it was in the Greek play, and gives a different force to the competing claims about 'civilisation'. The shared Yoruba identity among the warring parties does not preclude repeated attempts to differentiate between civilised and barbarian. In scene four, after the encounter between Anlugbua and Lawumi, Gesinde, the Talthybios-figure, reprimands the Owu when he thinks that the women are setting fire to their tents (26):

We Ijebus are civilised, and
Have our code of conduct: we will not allow bush people
To embarrass us with any barbaric act of self-destruction.

This dismissive attitude is quite remarkable when we recall that in the Greek, Talthybios' worry was that the women's nobility would get him into trouble, not their baseness (301-3). Not that he gets it all his own way; addressing Orisaye, the Kassandra-figure, the chorus leader asks her not to embarrass the women, and not to make 'your poor mother/Shake before these barbarians' (29). The Owu and the Ijebu, then, do not need differences of skin colour or continent to be able to call each other barbarian.[91]

Given these interchangeable insults, and the revision of categories envisaged by the guilt of the Owu, what happens to 'Kassandra's paradox'? Like the Greek Kassandra, Orisaye is termed mad by her mother and her companions (26, 28) but here she makes it quite clear that she is not. She sings and dances deliriously (28), but she knows full well that there is no cause for a celebration; she speaks of sorrow and fear (27, 28). Yet she rejoices at her coming encounter with the Balogun (the counterpart to Agamemnon), not because of some delusion about her status as a concubine, but simply because she plans to cut his throat (29). Well aware that after this she will die, she also knows what is in store for the Ijebu. Most of them will not get home, and those that do will find their lands invaded by others, and will suffer 'a defeat worse than our own', whereas the Owu can 'Dance ... for the victory that is coming!' (30). Although we may not need much prompting to recognise Kassandra's paradox, it is subtly altered by the fact that in the relay of aggression between the parties to the siege, the Owu have already enjoyed a victory, and have themselves razed a city to the ground.

In the calm after the storm of Orisaye's scene, the women, like their Greek counterparts, look for ways to understand their predicament. They focus on the gods' apparent abandonment of them, with Erelu concluding that 'we have always been alone, my dear women. Only/We did not know it' and that 'Each of us has become our own god' (33). As they remember the night that Owu fell – only last night – Erelu concludes that happiness is a mask that the gods use to trick humans, who 'have no defence' against the 'pettiness' of divinity (37). While Greek Hekabe must similarly work through a series of different responses to

divinity, the conclusions articulated here by the chorus leader
are more inclined to indict humanity (37):

> … we never remember that, we human beings.
> We are always eager to forget that the sky is at its calmest
> In the moments before a mighty thunderstorm.

The conclusions about human responsibility – the 'lesson'
rather than the 'law' – are perhaps less stressed in *Trojan
Women*.

In a departure from the Greek play, a day passes before the
following scene, spent by the women 'stinking in our underwear'
and by the conquerors arguing over the loot (39). Distribution
of the booty begins with the entry of the Andromache-figure,
Adumaadan, with her baby on her back, on her way to join her
new master. The scenes in which Aderogun (Astyanax) is taken
from his mother, and later mourned by his grandmother, are
pared down, as in Mee or McLaughlin. There is no long speech
from Adumaadan addressing her son or raging at her enemies,
and no stage business from the child, as in Sartre or Kennelly.
Adumaadan hands the baby over, then begs for him back, and
holds him while Gesinde describes, self-pityingly, how he will
feel when he has to 'bash/The child's head against a tree,/And
crush his skull as we've been ordered to do' (45). There is thus
no exploration of the mother's feelings, or of the child's understanding (he is in any case a baby here rather than a child), and
instead, Gesinde offers to disrupt the emotional and moral
balances still further when he observes that 'you'd do as much
/to us if your side won the war' (44). Given Osofisan's published
political and artistic allegiances, we might be inclined to type
these scenes as Brechtian, committed to making us think rather
than making us feel. We might also speculate that this play,
conscious as it is of its long lineage, chooses other grounds on
which to vie with the earlier versions – principally, I have
suggested, in making the people of Owu as culpable as their
assailants.

The 'guilt of the Owu' surfaces again in the following scene,

the *agôn* between the Hekabe and Helen-figures, who are here
Erelu Afin and Iyunloye. Like Helens before her, Iyunloye is
skilled with words (50) and uses impressive arguments, but
here she also very decidedly sets about seducing her husband
the Mayé (the Menelaos figure), admiring him physically and
flattering him with her tale of creating and selling textile
patterns based on his previous work (49, 53). As full of chutzpah
as the Greek Helen, she claims that contempt for her is contempt for the Mayé too (48) and that he should be grateful to
her for making him famous (49). She does not claim to have saved
'Greece', as she does in Euripides, but as we shall see later, she
does show an analogous political awareness. We are used to the
idea that 'Helen' will blame 'Hekabe' for raising her son instead
of destroying him at birth, and sure enough, Iyunloye does (51).
Although she trots out a number of other dusty old arguments
– that she tried numerous times to escape, that she was forced
into her various marriages (53) – it is notable that she does not
invoke in exoneration the power of the gods. Some of Iyunloye's
arguments are new; like the Greek Helen, she blames her
husband for being away when she was 'abducted', but in her
story – uncontradicted by Erelu Afin – she was taken away in a
general attack by Owu on the market at Apomu, and was forced
to barter her beauty for her life (51-2).

Erelu Afin counters the familiar arguments in familiar fashion, but when she launches into a description of how the
luxuries of Owu held Iyunloye spellbound, as Troy did Helen,
she meets with unexpected resistance. Iyunloye agrees that Ife
is 'backward', like Menelaos' Sparta, but goes on to draw quite
other conclusions (55):

> Without
> Our sweat and our labour in Ife, tell me, just where
> Would Owu be? Without the profits from our markets
> Which your warriors seize from our women;
> Without the yams and fruits you plunder from our farms,
> How would you feed? How would you be handsome
> Without the jewels beaten out of our bronze factories?

3. Twentieth-century Receptions

The relationships between the various Yoruba cities are now said to be not just those of mutual antagonism and assault, but of systemic exploitation, akin to the earlier charges of enslaving, where Owu is undoubtedly the aggressor. That this is a correct evaluation of the situation is made clear by Erelu Afin's angry response, which does not deny the charge in the least, but uses *force majeure* to claim instead (55):

> What are you saying? Don't divert the argument:
> It is the fate of the conquered to toil for the strong!
> That is the logic of war, the logic of defeat!

As in the Greek play, the defeated queen here uses the language of her conquerors. The specific words, 'the logic of war, the logic of defeat', were, as we have seen, uttered by Anlugbua in the first scene (7), and have since been repeated with minor variations by the Mayé (47) and by Gesinde (44, 59). In the mouths of the male characters they appear uncomplicatedly despicable, but what are we to think of them here? Arguments about the moral decline of the Euripidean Hekabe, in the Helen scene, are relatively familiar, but this play claims that Erelu Afin already belonged to a city that enslaved other Yoruba, and so makes a different and more damning argument about her moral stature. She is not simply employing any and all arguments to get Helen killed, as in the Greek, but is speaking from within a larger and perhaps more deadly power struggle. We should not overlook the fact that Erelu Afin speaks of herself as a conqueror. Her adoption here of the slogan about the logic of war seems to rework Kassandra's claim about victory and defeat, not to undermine the achievement of the victors, but to suggest that the vanquished themselves, for all their suffering, may not emerge uncompromised.

There are a few other significant changes made to the 'Helen' scene. General Okunade, the Mayé, is a figure quite different from Menelaos, because he used to be a creative artist. Renowned for his textile designs, he gave them up when his wife was stolen, to become instead a feared fighter. In place of the

131

back-and-forth of destruction that we have witnessed between the Owu and their enemies, the Mayé offers a
representation of change from one state to another – a partly
optimistic notion of human capacity even though on this
occasion the change is from creativity to destruction. Excessively pleased with his day and himself, the Mayé enters
triumphantly; like Menelaos he has been given absolute freedom to do what he wants with his wife, but there is an
alarming difference. Several versions of Menelaos, as in
Hartman, have relished the details of Helen's prospective
punishment at the hands of Greek men, but Osofisan's general considers that he might (47)

> ... release her into the arms of the numerous women
> Turned into widows by this war, and
> Let them lynch her! Yes!
> Or – even better still –
> Give her to the children grieving inconsolably
> Over the loss of their fathers.

The play thus calmly envisages Iyunloye's death at the hands
of women and children, the very people that we are busy
representing to ourselves as victims. What actually happens to
Iyunloye is, of course, something completely different. As in the
Mee, the irony of the situation is savoured to its logical conclusion, for 'Menelaos' and 'Helen' are fully reunited before they get
home. Gesinde explains to the women later (61):

> If I may inform you, beauty
> Has conquered once again, as before. That celebrated slut
> Has regained Mayé's heart, and joined his caravan.

This announcement is devastating for the women of Owu, and
it very tellingly can also be subsumed under 'the logic of vic-
tory/the logic of defeat ... the justice of the great ' (61). By now,
however, the shifting moral compass may incline us merely to
be glad that somebody escapes the carnage, and perhaps also

that the Ijebu women and children are not invited in their turn
to serve as executioners.

In between the 'Helen' scene and the news of Iyunloye's
vindication comes the burial of Aderogun, wrapped in his father's war-dress. As was his parting from his mother, his
funeral is brief; Erelu makes only a short speech, less than half
the length of the Greek counterpart, and the work of the lamentation is carried by the chorus women, speaking in turn rather
than chorally. Drawing on Sartre rather than the Greek, the
play describes Adumaadan's new husband, the Otunba, as a
'sensitive' man who realises that to have the war-dress 'hanging
in his bedchamber among his other/War trophies might upset
Adumaadan' (59). His sensitivity is not contradicted by the fact
that 'he gave the orders to kill the child' (59). This kind of
collocation is 'the logic of war, the law of defeat' (59), and here
we may see a slightly new inflection of the now-familiar slogan.
It may be that the Otunba, in his enforced role as infanticide,
suffers from this 'law' and 'logic' as much as does the dead child.

Why Erelu Afin does not make a long speech over her grandson's body may be because she is being saved for another task,
which becomes clear only when Gesinde announces the final
burning of the city (61). What Erelu must do is something that
only she is qualified for; in the absence of the men of Owu, she
is the only one trained to 'release their spirits and send them
back/Safely home to the ancestors' (62). Although she demurs,
feeling too weak, she eventually agrees to go through with the
rite, and after a series of hesitations and interruptions the rite
is performed, the songs sung, Erelu entranced and possessed by
Anlugbua. We might now imagine that the spirits are released
and the ancestors consoled, but we would be wrong. When
Anlugbua possesses Erelu, so that she speaks with his voice, he
explains that the humans have put themselves beyond the
range of the gods' help.

Anlugbua is not exactly a *deus ex machina*, because he is
summoned by the ritual performance of the women, who need
him to help them to 'save our future from eternal damnation'
(62) and to 'find our way back in the void' (65). Just like a *deus*

ex machina, however, he explains, judges and foretells the future. In Sartre, Poseidon's closing indictment took in all humanity when he accused it of ravaging fields and cities, violating temples and tombs, and torturing the vanquished (80). Here, in a remarkable move, Anlugbua places the blame for the Owu conflict specifically on the suffering slaves before him. As if they represent the entire city of Owu, he addresses them (65):

> You were given this life. You chose to waste it
> In a senseless quarrel over a woman –

To this extraordinary accusation, Erelu replies with the extraordinary rejoinder that they were just following orders (65) – an admission of guilt here just as much as when Gesinde used it in relation to Aderogun (45). For this guilt there must be a penalty, beyond the loss of the city that has been endured, and not just for this specific guilt but for the larger human failing of not learning from history, or worse still, of rewriting it (66). The women plead that they did not read or write the history, because they are its victims rather than its makers – a stance that is, in view of Lawumi's earlier narrative, questionable at least. The god advises a more proactive stance; not only should the victims train themselves to take over both the history and its telling, but they should learn 'the wisdom/of sticking together, and loving one another ...' (66). In this line the god has ceased entirely to be Euripidean, because he can envisage the kind of compassion that in Euripidean drama characterises the relationships of humans only, and offers them a defence against the machinations of the divine.[92] Here, it is the god who has to teach the humans their humanity.

Like Sartre's Poseidon, the god has the final word. The humans cannot escape the penalty of 'wandering and slavery' (66), but the god is moved by their plight, not least because gods too suffer from conflict (67). While Erelu dies, on stage, from her encounter with deity, the god can promise the rest of the city a kind of afterlife. Owu will rise again, but not as itself; instead,

134

the people will build new communities scattered over Yorubaland and in the other locations of slavery (67). This much salvation is all the god can provide in the teeth of the humans' 'ceaseless volition for self-destruction', their 'thirst for blood' and eagerness 'to devour one another' (67).

Although the ending thus involves images of slavery and diaspora, it does not evoke the full context of the colonial scramble for Africa; most of the slaves will remain in Yorubaland, and the white men, as we have seen, are represented as more or less a footnote to a Yoruba conflict. The play thus resists allotting blame along the lines of black and white, and instead indicts the women of Owu themselves, paradigmatic not simply as victims but also, for the purposes of this play, as aggressors. In this most contemporary version of *Trojan Women*, at the end of the tradition and the start of the century, the women of Owu take on the mantle of Greek tragedy, and achieve a fully mythic status, not simply by recalling the contours of the ancient play, but by being as culpable as anyone else in the relay of violent destructions.

Notes

Contexts

1. Shakespeare, *Hamlet* (Oxford: Oxford University Press, 1977) 2.2.562. My practice in transliterating names has been to use Greek spellings (Hekabe, Kassandra, Menelaos, Talthybios) except when a dramatist under discussion uses Hecuba, Cassandra, Menelaus, Talthybius etc. Greeks may also be called the Achaeans; Trojans are also known as Phrygians. I shall call the play *Trojan Women*, but its Greek name may also be rendered *Women of Troy* or *Troades*.

2. Kitto, *Greek Tragedy* (New York: Harper and Row, 1950) 218.

3. Renault, *Mask of Apollo* (London: Sceptre Books, 1986) 13-15.

4. See Scodel, *Trojan Trilogy* (Göttingen: Vandenhoeck and Ruprecht, 1980) 120 on the intensely intellectual qualities of the play.

5. Lee, *Euripides: Troades* (Basingstoke: Macmillan, 1976) xxvi.

6. All dates are BCE unless otherwise indicated.

7. *The Complete Greek Tragedies. Euripides III: Four Plays* (Chicago: Chicago University Press, 1958) 123.

8. Conacher, *Euripidean Drama* (Toronto: University of Toronto Press, 1967) 137 n. 18 lists the criticisms of the structure. For Lattimore, *Four Plays*, 124 it is shapeless and full of padding.

9. Murray, *The Trojan Women of Euripides* (London: G. Allen, 1905) 5-6. See Hall, 'Introduction' to James Morwood (ed.), *Euripides: The Trojan Women and Other Plays* (Oxford: Oxford University Press, 2001) xxiv for Schlegel's similar view and its dominance in the early part of the twentieth century. Poole, 'Total Disaster: Euripides' *Trojan Women*', *Arion* n.s. 3:3 (1976) 258, and Morwood, *Plays of Euripides* (London: Bristol Classical Press, 2002) 45 constitute variations on the theme.

10. Mossman, 'Women's Voices' in Gregory (ed.), *A Companion to Greek Tragedy* (Oxford: Blackwell Publishing, 2005) 357.

11. Dunn, *Tragedy's End* (Oxford: Oxford University Press, 1996) 101-14.

12. Hartigan, *Greek Tragedy on the American Stage* (Westport CT: Greenwood Press, 1995) 15.

13. Hartigan, *Greek Tragedy on the American Stage*, 153.

14. This phenomenon is investigated authoritatively in Hall, Macintosh and Wrigley (ed.), *Dionysus since 69: Greek Tragedy at the Dawn of the Third Millennium* (Oxford: Oxford University Press, 2004).

15. On the female voice in the play see especially Mossman, 'Women's Voices'.

16. *Dionysus since 69*, 9-18.

17. On the barbarian in the play see Croally, *Euripidean Polemic* (Cambridge: Cambridge University Press, 1994) 103-15.

18. See now Dué, *The Captive Woman's Lament in Greek Tragedy* (Austin TX: University of Texas Press, 2006), for a nuanced account of sympathy and identification.

19. On *Persians* see most recently Hall, *The Theatrical Cast of Athens* (Oxford: Oxford University Press, 2006) 184-224.

20. All translations are my own unless otherwise noted.

21. *Greek Tragedy and the British Theatre 1660-1914* (Oxford: Oxford University Press, 2005) ch. 17.

22. The beginning of democracy is traditionally ascribed to the reforms of Kleisthenes in 508/7.

23. See e.g. Thucydides 2.65, Aristophanes *Acharnians* 212.

24. Thucydides himself held a contract for gold mines in Thrace (4.105).

25. Hornblower, 'Greece: The History of the Classical Period', 124-55 in Boardman, Griffin and Murray (ed.), *The Oxford History of the Classical World* (Oxford: Oxford University Press, 1986) 139.

26. Anaxagoras was prosecuted for impiety, apparently by the political enemies of Pericles (Plutarch *Pericles* 32).

27. The fragments of the sophists are collected in Diels-Kranz, and translated by Rosamund Sprague in *The Older Sophists* (Columbia: University of South Carolina Press, 1972). See also Dillon and Gergel, *The Greek Sophists* (London: Harmondsworth, 2003). A good introduction to the sophists' work is Kerferd, *The Sophistic Movement* (Cambridge: Cambridge University Press, 1981).

28. The best place to see this anxiety in action is probably the contest between Good and Bad Argument in Aristophanes' *Clouds*.

29. See Connor, 'City Dionysia and Athenian Democracy', *Classica et Mediaevalia* 40 (1989) 7-32, and the recent debate between Goldhill, 'The Great Dionysia and Civic Ideology', 97-129 in Winkler and Zeitlin (ed.), *Nothing to Do with Dionysos?* (Princeton: Princeton University Press, 1990), Rhodes, 'Nothing to Do with Democracy: Athenian Drama and the Polis', *Journal of the Hellenic Society* 123 (2003) 104-19, and Henderson, 'Drama and Democracy', in Loren J. Samons II (ed.), *The Cambridge Companion to the Age of Pericles* (Cambridge: Cambridge University Press, 2007).

30. On the nature of Dionysos and his connections to theatrical celebrations, see Seaford, *Dionysos* (London: Routledge, 2006).

31. See Goldhill, 'Great Dionysia', for the generals' role, and other extra-dramatic events that were part of the festival.

32. These matters are fully discussed by e.g. Cartledge, ' "Deep Plays": Theatre as Process in Greek Civic Life', 3-35 in Easterling (ed.), *The Cambridge Companion to Greek Tragedy* (Cambridge: Cambridge University Press, 1997), and Hall, 'The Sociology of Athenian Tragedy', 93-126, also in Easterling (ed.).

33. Aristotle *Poetics* 1449a20 is an important piece of evidence, but theories about the origins of Greek drama proliferate in the absence of information. See Csapo and Miller, *The Origins of Theater in Ancient Greece and Beyond* (Cambridge: Cambridge University Press, 2007).

34. See Halleran, *The Stagecraft of Euripides* (London and Sydney: Croom Helm, 1985) 94. The only other protagonist who is constantly on stage is Aeschylus' Prometheus. Medea, Oedipus at Colonus and Hekabe in *Hekabe* all have brief respites from the stage at some point.

35. On the messenger speech see de Jong, *Narrative in Drama* (Leiden and New York: E.J. Brill, 1991), especially ch. 3, and Goward, *Telling Tragedy* (London: Duckworth, 1999).

36. The *Acharnians* (426) includes a scene that parodies the *Telephus* (438). In *Women at the Thesmophoria* (411) the ending is made up of quickfire parodies of three Euripidean plays, *Helen*, *Andromeda* and *Palamedes*. *Frogs* (405) makes fun of lines by Aeschylus as well as by Euripides.

37. This is recorded in the ancient *Life* of Aeschylus. See Page, *Aeschyli Septem Quae Supersunt Tragoedias* (Oxford: Clarendon Press, 1972) 331-5.

38. For readings of Euripides' *Orestes* along these lines see e.g. Zeitlin, 'The Closet of Masks', *Ramus* 9 (1980) 51-77. The recognition scene in Euripides' *Elektra* has long been considered a parody of Aeschylus' *Libation Bearers*. The *agôn* in the *Frogs* of Aristophanes is constructed around the notion of a competition between Aeschylus and Euripides, both dead.

39. See Ober and Strauss, 'Drama, Political Rhetoric, and the Discourse of Athenian Democracy', 237- 70 in Winkler and Zeitlin (ed.).

40. See especially the *Frogs* and the poetic contest staged there, in which Euripides upsets the traditional Aeschylus with his many radical statements.

41. On Homer in *Trojan Women* see especially Davidson, 'Euripides, Homer and Sophocles', *Illinois Classical Studies* 24-5 (2002) 117-28, and 'Homer and Euripides' *Troades*', *Bulletin of the Institute of Classical Studies* 4 (2001) 65-79.

42. This account of tragedy is associated most closely with the work of Vernant and Vidal-Naquet. See especially *Myth and Tragedy in*

Ancient Greece (New York: Zone Books, 1988), and also Barlow *Trojan Women* (Warminster: Aris & Phillips, 1986) 4-5. Poole, 'Total Disaster', 276 has a slightly different account of the way that outmoded old values persist, in *Trojan Women*, to poison the present.

43. Walton, 'Introduction' to *Euripides Plays II: The Women of Troy*, trans. Don Taylor (London: Methuen, 1991) xviii.

44. Morwood, *Plays of Euripides*, 44, Dunn, *Tragedy's End*, 102.

45. See especially Scodel, *Trojan Trilogy*.

46. Stuttard, *An Introduction to Trojan Women* (Brighton: Company Dionysos, 2005) 32.

47. *Tragedy's End*, 101-14.

48. Melos, as a colony of Sparta, was governed as an oligarchy. According to Thucydides, the Athenian envoys were not permitted to speak to the mass of Melians but only to the rulers.

49. For introductions to the issue of Thucydidean speeches see Hornblower, *Thucydides* (London: Duckworth, 1987) 45-72, and Crane, *The Blinded Eye: Thucydides and the New Written Word* (Lanham MD: Rowman and Littlefield, 1996) 65-72. For different views of the relationship between the Melian Dialogue and contemporary rhetoric, see Finley, 'Euripides and Thucydides', *Harvard Studies in Classical Philology* 49 (1938) 23-68, Hudson-Williams, 'Conventional Forms of Debate and the Melian Dialogue', *American Journal of Philology* 71 (1950) 156-69, and Amit, 'The Melian Dialogue and History', *Atheneum* 56 (1968) 216-35.

50. This gap is repeatedly examined in *Trojan Women*, as in Kassandra's 'mad' speech and the *agôn* between Hekabe and Helen. See Goldhill, 'The Language of Tragedy', 127-50 in Easterling (ed.), 145-50, and Gregory, *Euripides and the Instruction of the Athenians* (Ann Arbor: University of Michigan Press, 1991) 170-4.

51. *A History of Ancient Greek Literature* (London: Heinemann, 1907), 7. Conacher, *Euripidean Drama*, 136 n. 17 lists such readers; see also Erp Taalman Kip, 'Euripides and Melos', *Mnemosyne* series 4 40.3-4 (1987) 414-19, and Rosenbloom, 'Empire and its Discontents: *Trojan Women, Birds*, and the Symbolic Economy of Athenian Imperialism', 245-72 in John Davidson, Frances Muecke and Peter Wilson (ed), *Greek Drama III: Essays in Honour of Kevin Lee* (London: Bulletin of the Institute of Classical Studies Supplement 87, 2006).

52. For changes in the Athenian notion of Troy throughout the fifth century, see Dué, *The Captive Woman's Lament*, 91-8, 113-14.

53. Scione suffered as Melos did in 421, and the land was given to the Athenian allies, the Plataeans. The inhabitants were restored by Sparta after the war (Plutarch *Lysander* 14).

54. See Croally, *Euripidean Polemic*, 57, quoting Pritchett, *The Greek State at War*, 5 vols (Berkeley CA: University of California Press, 1971-) vol. 5: 218.

55. Erp Taalman Kip, 'Euripides and Melos', 41.
56. Hamilton, *Euripides: Trojan Women* (New York: Bantam, 1971) 1.
57. Hartigan, *American Stage*, 15.
58. See e.g. Dué, *The Captive Woman's Lament*, 150.
59. Later avatars do, as in the case of Poseidon in Sartre's *Trojan Women*. See further below.
60. Croally, *Euripidean Polemic*, 234.
61. Murray, *Trojan Women*, 7; Poole, 'Total Disaster', 267.
62. Conacher, *Euripidean Drama*, 139.
63. On Aristotle's *Poetics* see especially Rorty, *Essays on Aristotle's Poetics* (Princeton NJ: Princeton University Press, 1992) and Halliwell, *Aristotle's Poetics* (London: Duckworth, 1986).
64. See Konstan, *Pity Transformed* (London: Duckworth, 2005) 72 on the structure of difference between self and other, as well as of identification, which Aristotle analyses as necessary to pity .

2. The Play

1. Easterling, 'Form and Performance', 151-77 in Easterling (ed.), 173.
2. I follow the line numbers of Barlow, *Trojan Women*.
3. In most accounts this is Ajax the Lesser rather than Ajax the son of Telamon. It is not completely clear whether Ajax is thought of as having raped Kassandra here. Hekabe still talks of her virginity (253-4), and Athena does not say explicitly that she was raped, but in other sources she most probably is.
4. For relevant bibliography see Croally, *Euripidean Polemic*, 128-9.
5. Hartigan, *American Stage*, 19 n.1.
6. Dunn, *Tragedy's End*, 108 notes that sententious utterances like the closing lines from Poseidon are usually reserved for the *deus ex machina*. Dyson and Lee, 'The Funeral of Astyanax in Euripides' *Troades*', *Journal of Hellenic Studies* 120 (2000) 17-33 at 17 argue from this that Poseidon's statement has special weight, and that the 'funeral' for Astyanax, on which more later, illuminates and even enacts it.
7. Of the later receptions of *Trojan Women*, Osofisan's *Women of Owu* goes furthest in this direction, as we shall see below.
8. *Tragedy and Athenian Religion* (Lanham MD: Lexington Books, 2003) 350, 353, 358, 360.
9. Conacher, *Euripidean Drama*, 139.
10. Poole, 'Total Disaster', 264-5.
11. e.g. Conacher, *Euripidean Drama*, 137, 139.
12. Others share this discourse, e.g. the chorus at 937-41.
13. I give a literal translation of the words; *achoreutos*, without dances or undanced, connects to the activity of singing too, through the figure of the chorus.

14. Gregory, *Instruction*, 162 notes that Hekabe still thinks of herself as leader of a community.

15. E.g. Morwood, *Plays of Euripides*, 44, Scodel, 'The Captive's Dilemma: Sexual Acquiescence in Euripides *Hecuba* and *Troades*', *Harvard Studies in Classical Philology* 98 (1998) 137-54.

16. See Scodel, *Trojan Trilogy*, 119.

17. On the various opinions see Croally, *Euripidean Polemic*, 107.

18. Polyxena in *Hekabe* cannot stand to live as a slave and welcomes her death at Achilles' tomb. In Berlioz's *Les Troyens* the women of Troy do all kill themselves, under the leadership of Cassandra, except for a very few who do not seem to have the work's sympathy.

19. See Croally, *Euripidean Polemic*, 107.

20. Stuttard, *Introduction to Trojan Women*, 60-1 rewrites Talthybios as an Everyman figure, a version of 'us' caught inside the play. In Kennelly and Hartman the herald is particularly sympathetic; contrast the self-pitying Gesinde in Osofisan's *Women of Owu* (45).

21. See Stuttard, *Introduction to Trojan Women*, 47 on this element of the invited identification.

22. Croally, *Euripidean Polemic*, 122-34 discusses the nature of victory in the play.

23. '*Trojan Women*: An Ancient Music Drama?', 103-23 in Stuttard and Shasha (ed.), *Essays on Trojan Women* (London: Actors of Dionysos, 2001) 111.

24. Rutherford, 'The Cassandra Scene', 90-103 in Stuttard and Shasha (ed.), *Essays*.

25. See Craik, 'Sexual Imagery and Innuendo in *Troades*', 1-15 in Powell (ed.), *Euripides, Women and Sexuality* (London: Routledge, 1990) on the sexual expressions in this scene. Stuttard, *Introduction to Trojan Women*, 57-8 claims that Kassandra's extremely sexualised language in his version of the play points up the Greeks' violence and asserts her own control of the situation. Many critics comment on the motif of marriage within the play; see e.g. Croally, *Euripidean Polemic*, 86-97, McCallum-Barry, '*Trojan Women*: Sex and the City', 74-90 in Stuttard and Shasha (ed.), *Essays*.

26. Barlow, *Trojan Women*, 174, Sourvinou-Inwood, *Tragedy and Religion*, 351.

27. Lee, *Troades* 125.

28. Gregory, *Instruction*, 163, 164

29. Mossman, 'Women's Voices', 359.

30. Vernant and Vidal-Naquet, *Myth and Tragedy*, 43.

31. Poole, 'Total Disaster', 276 suggests that Kassandra's speech 'resurrects' heroism.

32. Subsequent dramatists have augmented these lines in order to elaborate character clashes; see Sartre, *Trojan Women*, xii, and Stuttard, *Introduction to Trojan Women*, 56 and 58.

33. On such readings see Lattimore, *Four Plays*, 124, Barlow, *Trojan Women*, 190, and Scodel, *Trojan Trilogy*, 11.

34. See Goldhill, 'Language', 149.

35. Gregory, *Instruction*, 165, 167.

36. The argument about self-consciousness, which is supported by the other women characters, is dependent on retaining 634-5, which some editors omit.

37. On Hekabe's inconsistencies here see e.g. Mossman, 'Women's Voices', 359.

38. Mossman, 'Women's Voices', 361 suggests that women in Greek drama generalise, usually in pious fashion, because they are talking in the presence of men, whereas in her long speech on marriage Andromache no longer cares what she says because there are no men left. It is the more excruciating, then, that she must guard her tongue after sentence is passed on her son.

39. *habra*, delicate, 821, *drosoenta*, dewy, 833. The latter may also recall the washing places where Hektor runs from Achilles in *Iliad* 22.150-6.

40. Useful recent treatments include Croally, *Euripidean Polemic*, 134-62 and Goldhill, 'Language', 145-50.

41. See e.g. Hazel, 'Women's Voices, Women's Hands', 20-30 in Stuttard and Shasha (ed.). Several twentieth-century versions of the play make far more of this point than even *Trojan Women* itself.

42. On Euripidean *agônes* see especially Lloyd, *The Agon in Euripides* (Oxford: Oxford University Press, 1992) and Collard, 'Formal Debates in Euripides' Drama', *Greece & Rome* 22 (1975) 58-71. On the frustrating qualities of this *agôn* see Stinton, *Euripides and the Judgement of Paris* (London: Society for the Promotion of Hellenic Studies Supplement 11, 1965) 36-9.

43. See Michelini, *Euripides and the Tragic Tradition* (Madison WI: University of Wisconsin Press, 1987) 171-2 on how these alternatives relate to the *agôn* as a whole, especially its discussion of responsibility.

44. Hall, *Theatrical Cast*, 314 makes the point that 'this cynical rhetorician' is the only woman in Troy who does not sing, i.e. who is not as emotional as the other women.

45. On Menelaos here see Lloyd, *Agon*, 111-12.

46. Lloyd, *Agon*, 101

47. See e.g. Barlow, *Trojan Women*, 205-6.

48. Lloyd, *Agon*, 101. Gorgias wrote an 'Encomium of Helen' in which appear versions of the arguments here. The dates are uncertain. See Goldhill, 'Language',145-50, and Michelini, *Tradition*, 158.

49. See Dover, 'Who is to Blame?', 1-9 in Stuttard and Shasha (ed.) 6-7, Michelini, *Tradition*, 174, Poole, 'Total Disaster', 274.

50. 'Who is to Blame?', 6-7.

51. The Greek of 975 is disputed, but the conflicting readings lead

to similar conclusions. See e.g. Barlow, *Trojan Women*, 212, Lloyd, *Agon*, 105-6.

52. This kind of very precise if paradoxical concern with technicalities of language was characteristic of sophistic enquiry. See e.g. Kerferd, *Sophistic Movement*, 68-77. Mossman, 'Women's Voices', 362 notes that Hekabe has no rhetorical markers in her part of the *agôn*, despite her apparently sophistic leanings.

53. Along these lines see Hazel, 'Women's Voices'.

54. E.g. Lee, *Troades*, 220, Curry, *Euripides: The Trojan Women* (London: Methuen, 1966) 9-10, Poole, 'Total Disaster', 273, Burnett, 'Trojan Women and the Ganymede Ode', *Yale Classical Studies* 25 (1977) 291-316, 293, 295.

55. On Euripides' alleged penchant for displaying heroes in rags see Aristophanes *Acharnians* 412-32.

56. See Barlow, *Trojan Women*, 207, Lloyd, *Agon*, 105.

57. Adulteresses at Athens were punished by exclusion from religious festivals, and if they infringed this rule could be attacked, but not killed. See Demosthenes, *Against Neaira*, 86.

58. Gregory, 'Comic Elements in Euripides', 59-75 in Cropp et al. (ed.), *Euripides and Tragic Theatre in the Later Fifth Century* (Champaign IL: Stipes Publishing for University of Illinois, 2000) (= *Illinois Classical Studies* 1991-2000) 69-72.

59. Lee, *Troades*, 228.

60. Lee, *Troades*, xxiii, Dover, 'Who is to Blame?', 4.

61. Barlow, *Trojan Women*, 205.

62. Gregory, *Instruction*, 174.

63. See Lloyd, *Agon*, 112, Croally, *Euripidean Polemic*, 157. Croally (158) makes the further point that we cannot know for certain that *this* Helen will enjoy the future mapped out by the Helen of the *Odyssey*.

64. Lee, *Troades*, 256.

65. Pentheus' mother Agave grieves over his body in the *Bacchae*, but Pentheus is, even if unsatisfactorily, an adult.

66. 'Most tragic', *tragikôtatos*, is Aristotle's word for Euripides (*Poetics* 1453a).

67. Hall, 'Introduction' to Hall, Macintosh and Wrigley, 17.

68. Dyson and Lee, 'Astyanax', 25.

69. She is not, however, like the founders of rituals in other Euripidean plays, because she cannot look to any kind of future. She is perhaps most like Agave in *Bacchae*, who collects her son's limbs for proper burial. On ritual disorder see Croally, *Euripidean Polemic*, 75-7; on ritual improvisation, Goff, 'Improvising on the Athenian Stage: Women's Ritual Practice in Drama', 79-91 in Angeliki Tzanetou and Marylin Parca (ed.), *Finding Persephone* (Champaign IL: University of Illinois Press, 2007).

70. Germane is the observation of Rosenbloom, 'Empire', 263, that

Astyanax's burial and lament reconstruct the aristocratic household at the moment of its extinction.

71. Segal, *Euripides and the Poetics of Sorrow: Art, Gender and Commemoration in Alcestis, Hippolytus and Hecuba* (Durham NC and London: Duke University Press, 1993) 30.

72. Dyson and Lee, 'Astyanax', 24 suggest that 'the child's age is variable between scenes'.

73. Segal, *Euripides and the Poetics of* Sorrow, 30. See also Poole, 'Total Disaster', 280, who notes the importance of the empty space that would have been filled by Hektor's 'full heroic presence'. 'Astyanax's little body ... at the centre of this play' paradoxically leaves this space 'vacant'.

74. Poole in 'Total Disaster' famously calls the play 'Euripides' Endgame'.

75. Stuttard, *Introduction to Trojan Women*, 61 suggests that the women do not in fact go to the ships, but really do immolate themselves in the flames of Troy.

76. Stuttard, *Introduction*, 37.

77. Critics agree that the ending of *Iphigenia at Aulis* is not by Euripides, but it is nonetheless thoroughly Euripidean. See Foley, *Ritual Irony* (Ithaca NY: Cornell University Press, 1985) 67.

3. Twentieth-century Receptions

1. I acknowledge here a debt to Willis, 'Euripides' *Trojan Women*: a twentieth century war play in performance' (unpublished DPhil thesis, Oxford, 2005), a study of twentieth-century performances, which discusses many productions that I have not been able to consider. The APGRD database also remains an invaluable tool.

2. Hall, 'Towards a Theory of Performance Reception' (*Arion* 21.1 2004, 51-89) 68-71 writes about the way in which memory can resist the 'ephemeral' quality of theatrical performance. She acknowledges that such memory is often private, which is the aspect that makes it difficult to recapture performance in such a way that it can be independently critiqued by those who have not witnessed it.

3. See e.g. Michelini, *Tradition*.

4. Hall and Macintosh, *British Theatre*, ch. 17, show that Murray was the first critic to link *Trojan Women* firmly to political comment on contemporary warfare. The most recent such linking is probably the 2007 production at the National Theatre, London, directed by Katie Mitchell, which invokes the invasions of Iraq as well as World War II. See e.g. http://www.nationaltheatre.org.uk/Women%20of%20Troy%3A%20D ominic%20Cavendish%20talks%20to%20the%20creative%20team+ 31166.twl.

5. For this history see Smith and Toynbee, *Gilbert Murray: An Unfinished Autobiography* (London: Allen and Unwin, 1960), Hartigan, *American Stage*, 15-19.

6. Hartigan, *American Stage*, 15-16. See also Smith and Toynbee, *Gilbert Murray*, 165.

7. Smith and Toynbee, *Gilbert Murray*, 164-5.

8. APGRD Database, University of Oxford, ed. Amanda Wrigley, http://www.apgrd.ox.ac.uk/database.

9. Hartigan, *American Stage*, 63.

10. Sartre's version of the *Oresteia*, *The Flies* (*Les Mouches*), had been staged in 1943, in the middle of World War II. Cacoyannis directed a few productions, including one from the translation by Edith Hamilton, before making his film of *Trojan Women*. See APGRD database.

11. References to the text are to *The Trojan Women (Euripides)*, trans. Ronald Duncan (New York: Alfred A. Knopf, 1976).

12. It is quite ironic that Loraux criticises Sartre for precisely his translation practice, writing that Sartre's 'theatrical universe has usurped that of Euripides'. See *The Mourning Voice: An Essay on Greek Tragedy*, trans. Elizabeth Trapnell Rawlings (Ithaca NY and London: Cornell University Press, 2002) 5.

13. See Leonard, *Athens in Paris* (Oxford: Oxford University Press, 2005) 225. Much of Leonard's last chapter is concentrated on this play.

14. The classicist Pierre Vidal-Naquet was another intellectual who publicly denounced the use of torture. The anti-imperialism of Frantz Fanon was developed during this war.

15. On it see also Loraux, *Mourning Voice*, 4.

16. It is of course arguable that the Algerian war left a dreadful domestic legacy in which victor and vanquished are again hard to distinguish. In 1965, when Sartre's play was produced, the final outcome in Vietnam, in all its equivocations, could not be known. Leonard concludes that the death of God in this play represents 'the death of the West' (*Athens in Paris*, 224).

17. Serban's staging of Andromache's parting from her son is similar; see below.

18. It is possible that we could interpret this gesture as an example of neo-Nazi passion for order, but I think that the mere presence of the doomed child in the scene tilts the gesture towards the analysis of humanism that Leonard reads in the play as a whole. Here, then, Duncan's elaboration on the translation resonates with Sartre's doubts, if only by providing too ready an answer for them. The soldier could also perhaps be understood as an existentialist making the '*acte gratuite*' of freedom.

In Kennelly, Astyanax is given enough subjectivity to run away from the guards, but he is, of course, caught again (180).

19. It was produced during the 1960s and 1970s in Britain, Italy, Germany, Japan and Poland. See APGRD database.

20. McKinnon, *Greek Tragedy into Film* (Rutherford: Fairleigh Dickinson University Press, 1986) 82.

21. Canby, 'Trojan Women: Cacoyannis Presents a Star-Filled Drama', *New York Times*, 28 September 1971.

22. McKinnon, *Greek Tragedy*, 82.

23. http://www.nypl.org/research/lpa/mirrors/ref/lostcontinenttheatre. html.

24. Green, *The Revisionist Stage: American Directors Reinvent the Classics* (Cambridge and New York: Cambridge University Press, 1994) 48.

25. Willis, 'Euripides'*Trojan Women*', 154-7.

26. Green, *Revisionist Stage*, 48.

27. Green, *Revisionist Stage*, 48.

28. Carruthers and Yasunari, *The Theatre of Suzuki Tadashi* (Cambridge: Cambridge University Press, 2004) 126, quoting Suzuki.

29. Allain, *The Art of Stillness: The Theatre Practice of Tadashi Suzuki* (London: Methuen, 2002) 159.

30. Carruthers and Yasunari, *Suzuki Tadashi*, 126.

31. Joseph, Review of Euripides' *The Trojan Women*, translated by Nicholas Rudall, The Shakespeare Theatre, Washington DC, 23 March to 8 May 1999 (consulted via Didaskalia website, http://www.didaskalia.net/reviews/1999_03_23_01.html.

32. Joseph, Review of *Trojan Women*.

33. Carruthers and Yasunari, *Suzuki Tadashi*, 128.

34. Hartigan, *American Stage*, 48.

35. Emmanuel Rubin, 'Israel's Theatre of Dissent', *World Literature Today*, 1986: 239.

36. Rubin, 243

37. The APGRD shows a production of *The Common Chorus I* at the University of Leeds, directed by Sian Coombs, some time between 1992 and 1994. Part I is Harrison's second rewriting of the *Lysistrata*; his first was produced in Nigeria in the late 60s. See Byrne (ed.), *Tony Harrison: Loiner* (Oxford: Oxford University Press, 1997) 5-6. There is little criticism available of this play. Most recently, see David Carter, *The Politics of Greek Tragedy* (Bristol: Bristol Phoenix Press, 2007) 155-8.

38. Harrison, *Plays 4: The Oresteia, The Common Chorus (Parts I and II)* (London: Faber & Faber, 2002) 197.

39. Harrison, 'Bitter Tears', *Guardian*, Saturday 19 March 2005. http://arts.guardian.co.uk/features/story/0,,1441004,00.html.

40. Harrison, *Plays 4*, 192, 197.

41. A related perception by Harrison is that recorded in McDonald, *Ancient Sun, Modern Light* (New York and Oxford: Columbia Univer-

sity Press, 1991) 140: the universal 'doesn't stay universal unless it gets a diet of particulars'.

42. On notions of gender at Greenham see Roseneil, *Common Women, Uncommon Practices: The Queer Feminisms of Greenham* (London and NY: Cassell, 2000).

43. There are good arguments that the women were not only undefeated, but also shaped subsequent British political culture; see Roseneil, *Common Women*.

44. References to the text are to Harrison, *Plays 4.*

45. See particularly *Common Chorus I*, 200-3, 208, 231, 274. See Roseneil, *Common Women*, 243-4 on collusion between the Greenham women and the British soldiers, against the Americans.

46. It was presumably a gift to Harrison that Poseidon is also the name for an underwater nuclear missile (281).

47. These were structures of branches covered in plastic sheeting. See the oral history at http://www.iwm.org.uk/upload/package/22/greenham/Besly2.htm.

48. Fortunately, this iconic image had its own specificity; the child, Kim Phuc, survived her injuries and the war.

49. Byrne, *H v & O: The Poetry of Tony Harrison* (Manchester: Manchester University Press, 1998) 148-9, Rowland, *Tony Harrison and the Holocaust* (Liverpool: Liverpool University Press, 2001) 71.

50. On lesbianism at Greenham see Fairhall, *Common Ground: The Story of Greenham* (London and New York: I.B. Tauris, 2006) 187-8, Roseneil, *Common Women*. A series of images of Greenham, including those of webs, may be found at http://www.guardian.co.uk/yourgreenham.

51. 'Keening' is one of the very first kinds of 'female' utterance described in Harford and Hopkins, *Greenham Common: Women at the Wire* (London: The Women's Press, 1984) 15. Singing and chanting are also prominent parts of the Greenham repertoire.

52. On this song see Taplin, 'The Chorus of Mams', 171-84 in Byrne (ed.), 177.

53. The demotic monosyllable and its doggedly doggerel rhyming is, of course, a feature of Harrison's poetic technique in a number of works, including this one. See Woodcock, 'Classical Vandalism: Tony Harrison's Invective', *Critical Quarterly* 32 (1990) 50-65 at 55, and Rowland, *Holocaust*, 72 on the 'disconcerting placement of twentieth century atrocity within the iambic trimeter and tetrameter typical of nursery rhymes'.

54. Since the stage directions are not accessible to theatre audiences, they may come to different conclusions.

55. In Euripides, the chorus have the last word. Compare the endings of Kennelly, who gives an immense closing speech to Hecuba, Hartman, whose Hecuba is turning into a dog, and Osofisan, who has Erelu Afin die before the end.

56. Critical treatments include McDonald, 'Rebel Women: Brendan Kennelly's Versions of Irish Tragedy', *New Hibernia Review* 9.3 (2005) 123-36, Wilmer, 'Radical Reworkings: Prometheus, Medea and Antigone: Metaphors for Irish Rebellion and Social Change', *Didaskalia* 3.1 (1996), O'Rawe '(Mis)Translating Tragedy: Irish Poets and Greek Plays', *Theatre Ancient & Modern* (Classical Receptions in Late Twentieth-Century Drama and Poetry in English: The Open University Reception Project, 1999).

57. References in the text are to Brendan Kennelly, *When Then is Now: Three Greek Tragedies* (Tarset: Bloodaxe Books, 2006).

58. O'Rawe '(Mis)translating'.

59. Kennelly, *When Then is Now*, 138.

60. O'Rawe '(Mis)translating'.

61. McDonald, 'Rebel Women', 134.

62. This became devastatingly clear in the Balkan conflict of the 1990s, but recent discoveries have shown that organised rape was a feature of World War II as well. See Beevor, *The Fall of Berlin 1945* (London: Viking, 2002).

63. The ending of the Kennelly is extraordinarily prolonged. Hecuba beats on the earth and addresses the dead of Troy, with some assistance from the chorus, for three pages, and is left to soliloquise for another three (206-12).

64. This may also be why there is such an emphasis on dreams in the play, unprecedented in any other version. E.g. 149, 164, 173, 195, 196, 203, 210, 212.

65. http://www.charlesmee.org/html/about.html.

66. http://www.charlesmee.org/html/about.html.

67. http://www.charlesmee.org/html/trojan.html, 78. All references are to the text published on the web at http://www.charlesmee.org/html/trojan.html. I refer to the pages by the numbers that appear when the pages are printed; no page numbers appear on the website.

68. See e.g. http://theater2.nytimes.com/mem/theater/treview.html?res=9801E2D61339F930A35754C0A960958260, and http://www.austinchronicle.com/gyrobase/Issue/review?oid=oid%3A184085. The production of 2003 (http://www.curtainup.com/trojanwomenmee.html) seems to have omitted the second half of the play, also.

69. See e.g. Ben Brantley, 'An Epic War Resolved With a Gershwin Ditty', *New York Times*, 3 July 1996.

70. See e.g. Brantley 'An Epic War'.

71. See Rush Rehm, '*Supplices,* The Satyr Play: Charles Mee's *Big Love*', *American Journal of Philology* 123.1 (2002) 111-18, for some similar criticisms of another of Mee's remakings.

72. Bob Mondello, 'Women on the Verge', *Washington City Paper* 19.14 (2-8 April 1999).

73. Mondello, 'Women on the Verge'.

74. Ruth Thompson, 'Witnessing, Weeping and Outrage – Modern Contexts and Ancient Woes in Euripides' *The Trojan Women* at the State Theatre Company of South Australia, November 2004', *Didaskalia* 6.3 (2006).

75. http://www.thisislondon.co.uk/theatre/article-23422093-details/Daring+to+be+different/article.do

76. Charles Spencer, 'Women of Troy: Euripides All Roughed Up', *Telegraph*, 30 November 2007.

77. See Ellen McLaughlin, *The Greek Plays* (New York: Theatre Communications Group, 2005) 79-88 for an account. All references to the plays are taken from this volume.

78. See reviews at http://www.auroratheatre.org/reviews.php?prod_id=54.

79. References are to Karen Hartman, *Troy Women*, published in Caridad Svich (ed.), *Divine Fire* (New York: Back Stage Books, 2005) 25-68.

80. At least one critic, however, did find her mad. See Alexis Soloski, 'Classic Tale of Strength Retold with Modern Spirit', *Yale Herald*, January 1997.

81. At least one critic found this the least convincing song of all. See Soloski, 'Classic Tale'.

82. Budelmann, '*Trojan Women* in Yorubaland: Femi Osofisan's *Women of Owu*', 15-39 in Hardwick and Gillespie (ed.), *Classics in Post-Colonial Worlds* (Oxford: Oxford University Press, 2007) 15-16.

83. Gibbs, 'Osofisan's Dramaturgy in *Tegonni*', 79-88 in Sola Adeyemi (ed.), *Portraits for an Eagle: Essays in Honour of Femi Osofisan* (Bayreuth: Bayreuth African Studies, 2006) 84

84. Similarly, if the audience only *thinks* it knows the history; cf. *Reel Rwanda!* and the analysis of it in Dunton, 'Representations of Horror: The Rwandan Genocide and Femi Osofisan's "Reel, Rwanda!"' in *Portraits for an Eagle*.

85. References in the text are to Femi Osofisan, *Women of Owu* (Ibadan: University Press PLC, 2006).

86. Budelmann, 'Yorubaland', 17 n. 7 notes three main ways in which the structure of this play differs from that of *Trojan Women*, which include prominently the opening and closing scenes.

87. Budelmann, 'Yorubaland', 21-2.

88. Later on the attackers are 'Ijebu beasts' and 'animals from Ife' (110). Erelu likens herself to a common mongrel, 10, which not only recalls the type of animal imagery that Greek tragedy is obsessed by, but hints as to the normal end of her story in metamorphosis.

89. Here I differ in my emphasis from Budelmann's reading, e.g. 'Yorubaland', 21.

90. Glenda Dickerson, who wrote a *Trojan Women* set in Africa, opines that 'This is a Greek tale, but it is also an African tale, and it

becomes the story of slavery' ('Transforming Through Performing: Oral History, African-American Women's Voices and the Power of Theater', http://www.fathom.com/feature/122665/index.html (2002). In Osofisan the victims turn out to be the slavers, not simply the enslaved.

91. This element of the play moves it away from being a commentary on the invasions of Iraq, where differences of culture and religion, not to mention skin colour, were never very far from the surface.

92. Knox, 'The *Hippolytos* of Euripides', *Yale Classical Studies* 13 (1952) 1-31 sums up this aspect of Euripidean drama as the 'affirmation of purely human values in an inhuman universe'.

Guide to Further Reading

Texts and translations

The OCT (Oxford Classical Texts) edition of Euripides' *Trojan Women*, in *Euripides Fabulae II*, edited by James Diggle (Oxford: Oxford University Press, 1981) is the industry standard, but is suitable only for those very comfortable with reading ancient Greek. K.H. Lee, *Euripides: Troades* (London: Macmillan, 1976, reprinted London: Bristol Classical Press, 1997) provides text and notes, while Shirley A. Barlow, *Euripides Trojan Women* (Warminster: Aris & Phillips, 1986) provides text, facing translation, and notes. The Loeb of David Kovacs, *Euripides: Trojan Women, Iphigeneia among the Taurians, Ion* (Harvard: Harvard University Press) provides text and facing translation.

The translations of Barlow and Kovacs are readable aids to comprehension and make no claim to literary or theatrical quality. Similar are two very readily available translations in paperback, which do not offer the Greek text. John Davie, *Euripides: Electra and Other Plays* (Harmondsworth: Penguin, 1998) has a wide-ranging introduction and interpretive notes by Richard Rutherford. The translation is in prose, with a slightly irritating convention of putting sung lyrics in italics. There is a glossary and a chronology. James Morwood for Oxford World Classics, *Euripides: The Trojan Women and Other Plays* (Oxford: Oxford University Press, 2000) has a fine introduction by Edith Hall, a chronology, map and notes. It also supplies the Hypothesis to the *Alexandros*, the first play in the 'Trojan trilogy'. The translation is in prose, with sung lyrics indicated by shorter lines. It is quite close to the Greek with occasional awkwardnesses in the English. Also readily available is the translation by Richmond Lattimore in the series edited by David Grene and Lattimore, *The Complete Greek Tragedies. Euripides III: Four Plays* (Chicago: Chicago University Press, 1958) is poetic and metrical, readable but by now a bit dated.

The 1905 translation and introduction by Gilbert Murray has recently been made available in *Gilbert Murray's Euripides: The Trojan Women and Other Plays* (Exeter: Bristol Phoenix Press, 2005). There is a very informative introduction by James Morwood, who judges the translation 'very theatrical and performable' (xiv), although its poetic sensibilities are removed from many modern tastes, being Swinburnian and Victorian (ix-x). It omits both Andromache's invitation to cannibalism and the 'joke' about Helen's weight. Modern translations that aim specifically at performance include Neil Curry, *Euripides: The Trojan Women* (London: Methuen, 1966), which is by a practising poet, and Nicholas Rudall, *Euripides: The Trojan Women* (Chicago: Ivan R. Dee, 1999), in a series designed for contemporary production and study. These translations have both been staged, as has that of Kenneth McLeish, *After the Trojan War* (Bristol: Longdunn, 1995) which is lively but which keeps the distracting Greek exclamations Otototoee! Eah eah! Eeoh eeoh! David Stuttard produced an adaptation for his own company, Company Dionysus, which includes a personal and committed introduction that links the play explicitly to 'the context of 9/11' (*An Introduction to Trojan Women* [Brighton: Company Dionysus, 2005] 49).

Other translations with literary ambition include the more free and colloquial version by Don Taylor, *Euripides Plays III*, with introduction by J. Michael Walton (London: Methuen, 1991), and *Daughters of Troy*, translated by Mark Rudmann and Katharine Washburn (Philadelphia: University of Pennsylvania Press, 1998) in the Penn Greek Drama Series edited by David Slavitt and Palmer Bovie. This series claims to offer fresh literary translations for acting or reading. The translators' preface is very interesting, especially as it seems particularly irritated at the challenges presented by the play. Diskin Clay's version, *Euripides: The Trojan Women* (Newburyport: Focus, 2004) by 'Hellenist and poet' (32), is distinguished by a number of illustrations, a discussion of the Trojan tetralogy of 415, and a translation of Gorgias' *Encomium of Helen*.

Athenian drama

These books have made particularly important contributions to debates about Athenian drama generally.

Easterling, P.E., *The Cambridge Companion to Greek Tragedy* (Cambridge: Cambridge University Press, 1997).
Vernant, J.-P. and Pierre Vidal-Naquet, *Myth and Tragedy in Ancient Greece* (New York: Zone Books, 1988).
Winkler, J.J. and Froma Zeitlin, *Nothing to Do with Dionysos? Athenian Drama in its Social Context* (Princeton: Princeton University Press, 1990).
Zeitlin, Froma, *Playing the Other: Gender and Society in Classical Greek Literature* (Chicago: University of Chicago Press, 1996).

Euripides

Some of the more recent standard works on Euripides.

Burian, Peter (ed.), *Directions in Euripidean Criticism* (Durham NC: Duke University Press, 1985).

Cropp, Martin, Kevin Lee and David Sansone (ed.), *Euripides and Tragic Theatre in the Later Fifth Century* (Champaign IL: Stipes Publishing for University of Illinois, 2000) (= *Illinois Classical Studies* 1999-2000).

Dunn, Francis, *Tragedy's End: Closure and Innovation in Euripidean Drama* (Oxford: Oxford University Press, 1996).

Foley, Helene, *Ritual Irony* (Ithaca NY: Cornell University Press, 1985).

Gregory, Justina, *Euripides and the Instruction of the Athenians* (Ann Arbor: University of Michigan Press, 1991).

Halleran, Michael, *The Stagecraft of Euripides* (London and Sydney: Croom Helm, 1985).

Lloyd, Michael, *The Agon in Euripides* (Oxford: Oxford University Press, 1992).

Michelini, Ann N., *Euripides and the Tragic Tradition* (Madison WI: University of Wisconsin Press, 1987).

Mossman, Judith (ed.), *Euripides* (Oxford: Oxford University Press, 2003).

Powell, Anton (ed.), *Euripides, Women and Sexuality* (London: Routledge, 1990).

Rabinowitz, Nancy, *Anxiety Veiled: Euripides and the Traffic in Women* (Ithaca NY: Cornell University Press, 1993).

Segal, Charles, *Euripides and the Poetics of Sorrow: Art, Gender and Commemoration in Alcestis, Hippolytus and Hecuba* (Durham NC and London: Duke University Press, 1993).

Trojan Women

A selection of important books and articles on the play.

Barlow, Shirley A., *Euripides Trojan Women* (Warminster: Aris & Phillips, 1986).

Croally, Neil, *Euripidean Polemic: The Trojan Women and the Function of Tragedy* (Cambridge: Cambridge University Press, 1994).

Burnett, Anne Pippin, 'Trojan Women and the Ganymede Ode', *Yale Classical Studies* 25 (1977): 291-316.

Poole, Adrian, 'Total Disaster: Euripides' Trojan Women', *Arion* n.s. 3:3 (1976) 257-87.

Murray, Gilbert, *The Trojan Women of Euripides, translated into*

English rhyming verse with explanatory notes (London: G. Allen, 1905).

Scodel, Ruth, *The Trojan Trilogy of Euripides* (Göttingen: Vandenhoeck and Ruprecht, 1980).

Stuttard, David and Tamsin Shasha, *Essays on Trojan Women* (London: Actors of Dionysos, 2001).

Reception

Books that deal with issues in classical reception and the reception of Greek tragedy.

Hall, Edith, Fiona Macintosh and Amanda Wrigley (ed.), *Dionysus Since 69: Greek Tragedy at the Dawn of the Third Millennium* (Oxford: Oxford University Press, 2004).

Hardwick, Lorna and Carol Gillespie (ed.), *Classics in Post-Colonial Worlds* (Oxford: Oxford University Press, 2007).

Hartigan, Karelisa, *Greek Tragedy on the American Stage: Ancient Drama in the Commercial Theater 1882-1994* (Westport CT: Greenwood Press, 1995).

Martindale, Charles and Richard Thomas, *Classics and the Uses of Reception* (Oxford: Blackwell, 2006).

McDonald, Marianne, *Ancient Sun, Modern Light* (New York and Oxford: Columbia University Press, 1991).

Bibliography

Allain, Paul, *The Art of Stillness: The Theatre Practice of Tadashi Suzuki* (London: Methuen, 2002).

Amit, M., 'The Melian Dialogue and History', *Atheneum* 56 (1968) 216-35.

Barlow, Shirley A., *Euripides Trojan Women* (Warminster: Aris & Phillips, 1986).

Bartow, Arthur, *The Director's Voice: 21 Interviews* (NY: Theatre Communications Group, 1988).

Beevor, Anthony, *The Fall of Berlin 1945* (London: Viking, 2002).

Boardman, John, Jasper Griffin and Oswyn Murray (ed.), *The Oxford History of the Classical World* (Oxford: Oxford University Press, 1986).

Brantley, Ben, 'An Epic War Resolved With a Gershwin Ditty', *New York Times*, 3 July 1996.

Budelmann, Felix, '*Trojan Women* in Yorubaland: Femi Osofisan's *Women of Owu*', 15-39 in Hardwick and Gillespie (ed.).

Burnett, Anne Pippin, '*Trojan Women* and the Ganymede Ode', *Yale Classical Studies* 25 (1977): 291-316.

Byrne, Sandie (ed.), *Tony Harrison: Loiner* (Oxford: Oxford University Press, 1997).

Byrne, Sandie, *H v & O: The Poetry of Tony Harrison* (Manchester: Manchester University Press, 1998).

Canby, Vincent, 'Trojan Women: Cacoyannis Presents a Star-Filled Drama', *New York Times*, 28 September 1971 (http://movies.nytimes.com/movie/review?res=9E03E3DB1338EF34BC4051 DFBF66838A669EDE

Carruthers, Ian, and Takahashi Yasunari, *The Theatre of Suzuki Tadashi* (Cambridge: Cambridge University Press, 2004).

Carter, David, *The Politics of Greek Tragedy* (Bristol: Bristol Phoenix Press, 2007).

Cartledge, Paul, ' "Deep Plays": Theatre as Process in Greek Civic Life', 3-35 in Easterling (ed.) 1997.

Collard, Christopher, 'Formal Debates in Euripides' Drama', *Greece & Rome* 22 (1975) 58-71.

Bibliography

Conacher, Desmond, *Euripidean Drama: Myth, Theme and Structure* (Toronto: University of Toronto Press, 1967).

Connor, W., 'City Dionysia and Athenian Democracy', *Classica et Mediaevalia* 40 (1989) 7-32.

Craik, Elizabeth, 'Sexual Imagery and Innuendo in *Troades*', 1-15 in Powell (ed.) 1990.

Crane, Gregory, *The Blinded Eye: Thucydides and the New Written Word* (Lanham MD: Rowman and Littlefield, 1996).

Croally, Neil, *Euripidean Polemic: The Trojan Women and the Function of Tragedy* (Cambridge: Cambridge University Press, 1994).

Cropp, Martin, Kevin Lee and David Sansone (ed.), *Euripides and Tragic Theatre in the Late Fifth Century* (Champaign IL: Stipes Publishing for University of Illinois, 2000) (= *Illinois Classical Studies* 1991-2000).

Csapo, Eric and Margaret Christina Miller, *The Origins of Theater in Ancient Greece and Beyond: From Ritual to Drama* (Cambridge: Cambridge University Press, 2007).

Curry, Neil, *Euripides: The Trojan Women* (London: Methuen, 1966).

Davidson, John, 'Homer and Euripides' *Troades*', *Bulletin of the Institute of Classical Studies* 4 (2001) 65-79.

Davidson, John, 'Euripides, Homer and Sophocles', *Illinois Classical Studies* 24-5 (2002) 117-28.

De Jong, Irene J.F., *Narrative in Drama: The Art of the Euripidean Messenger-speech* (Leiden and New York: E.J. Brill, 1991).

Dickerson, Glenda, 'Transforming Through Performing: Oral History, African-American Women's Voices and the Power of Theater', http://www.fathom.com/feature/122665/index.html (2002).

Diels, Hermann and Walter Kranz, *Die Fragmente der Vorsokratiker: griechisch und deutsch* (Zurich and Berlin: Weidmann, 1964).

Dillon, John and Tania Gergel, *The Greek Sophists* (London: Harmondsworth, 2003).

Dover, Kenneth, 'Who is to Blame?' 1-9 in Stuttard and Shasha (ed.).

Dué, Casey, *The Captive Woman's Lament in Greek Tragedy* (Austin TX: University of Texas Press, 2006).

Dunn, Francis, *Tragedy's End: Closure and Innovation in Euripidean Drama* (Oxford: Oxford University Press, 1996).

Dunton, Chris, 'Representations of Horror: the Rwandan Genocide and Femi Osofisan's "Reel, Rwanda!"', in Sola Adeyemi (ed.), *Portraits for an Eagle: Essays in Honour of Femi Osofisan* (Bayreuth: Bayreuth African Studies, 2006).

Dyson, M. and K.H. Lee, 'The Funeral of Astyanax in Euripides' *Troades*', *Journal of Hellenic Studies* 120 (2000) 17-33.

Easterling, P.E. (ed.), *The Cambridge Companion to Greek Tragedy* (Cambridge: Cambridge University Press, 1997).

Easterling. P.E. , 'Form and Performance', 151-77 in Easterling (ed.).

Bibliography

Erp Taalman Kip, A. Maria van, 'Euripides and Melos', *Mnemosyne* series 4 40.3-4 (1987) 414-19.

Fairhall, David, *Common Ground: The Story of Greenham* (London and New York: I.B. Tauris, 2006).

Finley, John J., 'Euripides and Thucydides', *Harvard Studies in Classical Philology* 49 (1938) 23-68.

Foley, Helene, *Ritual Irony* (Ithaca NY: Cornell University Press, 1985).

Gibbs, James, 'Osofisan's Dramaturgy in *Tegonni*', 79-88 in Sola Adeyemi (ed.), *Portraits for an Eagle: Essays in Honour of Femi Osofisan* (Bayreuth: Bayreuth African Studies, 2006).

Goff, Barbara, 'Improvising on the Athenian Stage: Women's Ritual Practice in Drama', 79-91 in Angeliki Tzanetou and Marylin Parca (ed.), *Finding Persephone* (Champaign IL: University of Illinois Press, 2007).

Goldhill, Simon, 'The Great Dionysia and Civic Ideology', 97-129 in Winkler and Zeitlin (ed.).

Goldhill, Simon, 'The Language of Tragedy: Rhetoric and Communication', 127-50 in Easterling (ed.).

Goward, Barbara, *Telling Tragedy: Narrative Technique in Aeschylus, Sophocles and Euripides* (London: Duckworth, 1999).

Green, Amy S., *The Revisionist Stage: American Directors Reinvent the Classics* (Cambridge and New York: Cambridge University Press, 1994).

Gregory, Justina (ed.), *A Companion to Greek Tragedy* (Oxford: Blackwell Publishing, 2005).

Gregory, Justina, *Euripides and the Instruction of the Athenians* (Ann Arbor: University of Michigan Press, 1991).

Gregory, Justina, 'Comic Elements in Euripides', 59-75 in Cropp et al. (ed.).

Hall, Edith, *Inventing the Barbarian: Greek Self-Definition through Tragedy* (Oxford: Oxford University Press, 1989).

Hall, Edith, 'Introduction' to James Morwood (ed.), *Euripides: The Trojan Women and Other Plays* (Oxford: Oxford University Press, 2001).

Hall, Edith, 'Towards a Theory of Performance Reception', *Arion* 21.1 (2004) 51-89.

Hall, Edith, *The Theatrical Cast of Athens: Interactions Between Ancient Greek Drama and Society* (Oxford: Oxford University Press, 2006).

Hall, Edith, ' Introduction: Why Greek Tragedy in the Late Twentieth Century?' 1-46 in Hall, Macintosh and Wrigley (ed.).

Hall, Edith, 'The sociology of Athenian tragedy', 93-126 in Easterling (ed.).

Hall, Edith and Fiona Macintosh, *Greek Tragedy and the British Theatre 1660-1914* (Oxford: Oxford University Press, 2005).

Bibliography

Hall, Edith, Fiona Macintosh and Amanda Wrigley (ed.), *Dionysus Since 69: Greek Tragedy at the Dawn of the Third Millennium* (Oxford: Oxford University Press, 2004).

Halleran, Michael, *The Stagecraft of Euripides* (London and Sydney: Croom Helm, 1985).

Halliwell, Stephen, *Aristotle's Poetics* (Chapel Hill: University of North Carolina Press, 1986).

Hamilton, Edith, *Euripides: Trojan Women* (New York: Bantam, 1971).

Hardwick, Lorna and Carol Gillespie (ed.), *Classics in Post-Colonial Worlds* (Oxford: Oxford University Press, 2007).

Harford, Barbara and Sarah Hopkins, *Greenham Common: Women at the Wire* (London: The Women's Press, 1984).

Harrison, Tony, *Plays 4: The Oresteia, The Common Chorus (Parts I and II)* (London: Faber & Faber, 2002).

Harrison, Tony, 'Bitter Tears', *Guardian*, Saturday 19 March 2005, http://arts.guardian.co.uk/features/story/0,,1441004,00.html.

Hartigan, Karelisa, *Greek Tragedy on the American Stage: Ancient Drama in the Commercial Theater 1882-1994* (Westport CT: Greenwood Press, 1995).

Hartman, Karen, *Troy Women*, published in Caridad Svich (ed.), *Divine Fire* (New York: Back Stage Books, 2005) 25-68.

Hazel, Ruth, 'Women's Voices, Women's Hands', 20-30 in Stuttard and Shasha (ed.).

Henderson, Jeffrey, 'Drama and Democracy', in Loren J. Samons II (ed.), *The Cambridge Companion to the Age of Pericles* (Cambridge: Cambridge University Press, 2007).

Hornblower, Simon, 'Greece: The History of the Classical Period', 124-55 in Boardman, Griffin and Murray (ed.).

Hornblower, Simon, *Thucydides* (London: Duckworth, 1987).

Hudson-Williams, H., 'Conventional Forms of Debate and the Melian Dialogue', *American Journal of Philology* 71 (1950) 156-69.

Joseph, Susan, Review of Euripides' *The Trojan Women*, translated by Nicholas Rudall, The Shakespeare Theatre, Washington DC, 23 March-8 May 1999, http://www.didaskalia.net/reviews/1999_03_23_01.html.

Kennelly, Brendan, *When Then is Now: Three Greek Tragedies* (Tarset: Bloodaxe Books, 2006).

Kerferd, G.B., *The Sophistic Movement* (Cambridge: Cambridge University Press, 1981).

Kitto, H., *Greek Tragedy* (New York: Harper and Row, 1950).

Knox, B.M.W., 'The *Hippolytos* of Euripides', *Yale Classical Studies* 13 (1952) 1-31.

Konstan, David, *Pity Transformed* (London: Duckworth, 2005).

Lee, K.H., *Euripides: Troades* (Basingstoke: Macmillan, 1976; reprinted London: Bristol Classical Press, 1997).

Bibliography

Leonard, Miriam, *Athens in Paris* (Oxford: Oxford University Press, 2005).

Lloyd, Michael, *The Agon in Euripides* (Oxford: Oxford University Press, 1992).

Loraux, Nicole, *The Mourning Voice: An Essay on Greek Tragedy*, trans. Elizabeth Trapnell Rawlings (Ithaca NY and London: Cornell University Press, 2002).

McCallum-Barry, Carmel, '*Trojan Women*: Sex and the City', 74-90 in Stuttard and Shasha (ed.); reprinted in Alan Beale (ed.), *Euripides Talks* (London: Bristol Classical Press, 2008) 116-25.

McDonald, Marianne, *Ancient Sun, Modern Light* (New York and Oxford: Columbia University Press, 1991).

McDonald, Marianne, 'Rebel Women: Brendan Kennelly's Versions of Irish Tragedy', *New Hibernia Review* 9.3 (2005) 123-36.

McKinnon, Kenneth, *Greek Tragedy into Film* (Rutherford: Fairleigh Dickinson University Press, 1986).

McLaughlin, Ellen, *The Greek Plays* (New York: Theatre Communications Group, 2005).

Menta, E., *The Magic World Behind the Curtain: Andrei Serban in American Theatre* (New York NY: Peter Lang, 1995).

Michelini, Ann N., *Euripides and the Tragic Tradition* (Madison WI: University of Wisconsin Press, 1987).

Mondello, Bob, 'Women on the Verge', Review of *The Trojan Women*, dir. JoAnne Akalaitis, *Washington City Paper* 19.14, 2-8 April 1999, http://www.washingtoncitypaper.com/display.php?id=17049

Morwood, James, *The Plays of Euripides* (London: Bristol Classical Press, 2002).

Morwood, James, *The Trojan Women and Other Plays* (Oxford: Oxford University Press, 2001).

Mossman, Judith, 'Women's Voices', 352-65 in Gregory (ed.).

Murray, Gilbert, *The Trojan Women of Euripides, Translated into English Rhyming Verse with Explanatory Notes* (London: G. Allen, 1905).

Murray, Gilbert, *A History of Ancient Greek Literature* (London: Heinemann, 1907).

O'Rawe, Des, '(Mis)Translating Tragedy: Irish Poets and Greek Plays', *Theatre Ancient & Modern* (Classical Receptions in Late Twentieth-Century Drama and Poetry in English: The Open University Reception Project, 1999), http://www2.open.ac.uk/ClassicalStudies/GreekPlays/Conf99/Orawe.htm.

Ober, Josiah and Barry Strauss, 'Drama, Political Rhetoric, and the Discourse of Athenian Democracy', 237- 70 in Winkler and Zeitlin (ed.).

Osofisan, Femi, *Women of Owu* (Ibadan: University Press PLC, 2006).

Page, D.L., *Aeschyli Septem Quae Supersunt Tragoedias* (Oxford: Clarendon Press, 1972)

Bibliography

Poole, Adrian, 'Total Disaster: Euripides' *Trojan Women*', *Arion* n.s. 3:3 (1976) 257-87.

Powell, Anton (ed.), *Euripides, Women and Sexuality* (London: Routledge, 1990).

Pritchett, Kendrick, *The Greek State at War*, 5 vols (Berkeley CA: University of California Press, 1971-).

Raeburn, David, '*Trojan Women*: An Ancient Music Drama?', 103-23 in Stuttard and Shasha (ed.).

Rehm, Rush, '*Supplices,* The Satyr Play: Charles Mee's *Big Love*', *American Journal of Philology* 123.1 (2002) 111-18.

Renault, Mary, *The Mask of Apollo* (London: Sceptre Books, 1986).

Rhodes, P.J. , 'Nothing to do with democracy: Athenian Drama and the Polis', *Journal of the Hellenic Society* 123 (2003) 104-19.

Rorty, Amelie Oksenberg (ed.), *Essays on Aristotle's Poetics* (Princeton NJ: Princeton University Press, 1992).

Rosenbloom, David, 'Empire and its Discontents: *Trojan Women, Birds*, and the Symbolic Economy of Athenian Imperialism', 245-72 in John Davidson, Frances Muecke and Peter Wilson (ed.), *Greek Drama III: Essays in Honour of Kevin Lee* (London: *Bulletin of the Institute of Classical Studies* Supplement 87, 2006).

Roseneil, Sacha, *Common Women, Uncommon Practices: The Queer Feminisms of Greenham* (London and NY: Cassell, 2000).

Rowland, Anthony, *Tony Harrison and the Holocaust* (Liverpool: Liverpool University Press, 2001).

Rubin, Emmanuel, 'Israel's Theatre of Dissent', *World Literature Today* (Spring 1986) 239-24.

Rutherford, Richard, 'The Cassandra Scene', 90-103 in Stuttard and Shasha (ed.); reprinted in Alan Beale (ed.), *Euripides Talks* (London: Bristol Classical Press, 2008), 126-33.

Sartre, J.-P., *Les Troyennes* (Paris: Editions Gallimard, 1965).

Sartre, J.-P., *The Trojan Women (Euripides),* trans. Ronald Duncan (New York: Alfred A. Knopf, 1976).

Scodel, Ruth, *The Trojan Trilogy of Euripides* (Göttingen: Vandenhoeck and Ruprecht, 1980).

Scodel, Ruth, 'The Captive's Dilemma: Sexual Acquiescence in Euripides *Hecuba* and *Troades*', *Harvard Studies in Classical Philology* 98 (1998) 137-54.

Seaford, Richard, *Dionysos* (London: Duckworth, 2006).

Segal, Charles, *Euripides and the Poetics of Sorrow: Art, Gender and Commemoration in Alcestis, Hippolytus and Hecuba* (Durham and London: Duke University Press, 1993).

Serban, Andrei, *The Greek Trilogy. Performances: Electra, Medea, The Trojan Women*, videotape of excerpts from the 1972-74 production (New York: Insight Media, 1991).

Shakespeare, William, *Hamlet* (Oxford: Oxford University Press, 1977).

Sidwell, Keith, 'Melos and the *Trojan Women*', 30-45 in Stuttard and Shasha (ed.).

Smith, Jean and Arthur Toynbee, *Gilbert Murray: An Unfinished Autobiography* (London: Allen and Unwin, 1960).

Sourvinou-Inwood, Christiane, *Tragedy and Athenian Religion* (Lanham MD: Lexington Books, 2003).

Spencer, Charles, 'Women of Troy: Euripides All Roughed Up', *Telegraph*, 30 November 2007,
http://www.telegraph.co.uk/arts/main.jhtml?xml=/arts/2007/11/30/bttroy130.xml

Sprague, Rosamund, *The Older Sophists: A Complete Translation by Several Hands of the Fragments in Diels-Kranz* (Columbia: University of South Carolina Press, 1972).

Stinton, T.C.W., *Euripides and the Judgement of Paris* (London: Society for the Promotion of Hellenic Studies Supplement 11, 1965).

Stuttard, David and Tamsin Shasha, *Essays on Trojan Women* (London: Actors of Dionysos, 2001).

Stuttard, David, *An Introduction to Trojan Women, Including an Adaptation of the Play* (Brighton: Company Dionysos, 2005).

Taplin, Oliver, 'The Chorus of Mams', 171-84 in Byrne ed.

Thompson, Ruth, 'Witnessing, Weeping and Outrage – Modern Contexts and Ancient Woes in Euripides' *The Trojan Women* at the State Theatre Company of South Australia, November 2004', *Didaskalia* 6.3 (2006),
http://www.didaskalia.net/issues/vol6no3/thompson.html

Vernant, J.-P. and Pierre Vidal-Naquet, *Myth and Tragedy in Ancient Greece* (New York: Zone Books, 1988).

Walton, J. Michael, 'Introduction' to *Euripides Plays II: The Women of Troy*, trans. Don Taylor (London: Methuen, 1991).

Willis, Avery T., 'Euripides' *Trojan Women*: a twentieth century war play in performance', unpublished DPhil thesis, Oxford, 2005.

Wilmer, Steve, 'Radical Reworkings: Prometheus, Medea and Antigone: Metaphors for Irish Rebellion and Social Change', *Didaskalia* 3.1 (1996),
http://www.didaskalia.net/issues/vol3no1/wilmer.html.

Woodcock, Bruce, 'Classical Vandalism: Tony Harrison's Invective', *Critical Quarterly* 32 (1990) 50-65.

Zeitlin, F.I., 'The Closet of Masks: Role Playing and Mythmaking in the *Orestes* of Euripides', *Ramus* 9 (1980) 51-77.

Glossary

agôn: contest or dispute; in tragedy, a set-piece debate between two speakers, usually acrimonious.

aretê: virtue, excellence or success.

choral ode: a song by the chorus; tragedies display several such songs at dramatic points in the action.

dactyl: a metrical unit consisting of one long syllable and two short. It is associated with the epic poetry of Homer.

demagogue: a leader of the people; usually a pejorative term with overtones of corruption and opportunism.

deus ex machina: 'God from the machine', indicating a divine character who appears at the end of a play from the mechane, i.e. borne in on a crane at roof height.

deuteragonist: second player; the actor who takes the second rank of characters.

ekkuklêma: a trolley or moving platform which entered the stage from the *skênê*-building bearing a tableau that displayed the effects of an action that took place indoors.

iamb: a metrical unit consisting of a short and a long syllable. Much dramatic poetry is written in iambic trimeter, with six iambs to a line. Iambic metre was considered by the Greeks to approximate the rhythm of speech.

leipô: I leave or abandon.

lyric: sung portions of a play, usually the chorus's part. Individual characters also have songs as well as spoken parts.

mêchanê: a crane that can bring divine characters on to the stage area at roof height.

orchêstra: dancing place, where the chorus perform.

parthenos: young girl, virgin.

peithô: persuasion.

phroudos: gone, disappeared.

polis: a 'city-state' or city, a self-governing unit that was the main form of community in classical Greece. The citizen body of the polis of Athens consisted of approximately 30,000 free adult males who were natives of the city.

prologue: the part of the play that precedes the entrance of the chorus.

protagonist: first actor, who takes the most important role(s).

rhêsis: a long speech in iambic metre, not sung, delivered by an actor.

scholiasts: very early critics and commentators on ancient texts, whose marginal remarks are preserved on early copies of texts.

skênê: the building at the back of the acting area in the ancient theatre.

sophist: a fifth-century intellectual and teacher, usually based in Athens even if non-Athenian, and usually questioning of traditional wisdom and morality.

sôphrosunê: modesty, chastity, prudence.

stephanos: crown or garland.

stichomythia: rapid exchange of single lines between two speakers; usually indicative of anger or distress.

stratêgos: general; ten generals were elected annually by the Athenians, but not by lot, since it was considered that the position of general required specific training and abilities.

tritagonist: third actor, who takes the smallest parts.

Chronology

BCE

Late 490s	Phyrnichos produces *Fall of Miletus*
480	Battle of Salamis: Persian invasion defeated by Greeks under Athenian leadership
c. 480	Euripides born
c. 462	Pericles begins career as leading politician at Athens
431	Peloponnesian War begins
430	Plague in Athens; death of Pericles
427	Fall of Plataea to Thebans
427	Cocyraean civil conflict
427	Revolt of Mytilene (Thucydides, Mytilenean Debate)
427	Arrival in Athens of Gorgias
416	Siege and sack of Melos; men executed, women and children enslaved (Thucydides, Melian Dialogue)
415	Sicilian expedition launched from Athens
415	*Trojan Women* produced, probably as part of trilogy including *Alexander* and *Palamedes*
412	Athenian naval disaster in Sicily
407/6	Death of Euripides
404	Peloponnesian War ends in defeat of Athens
384-322	Life of Aristotle, author of *Poetics* and *Rhetoric*
29-19	Vergil at work on *Aeneid*

CE

first century	Seneca's *Troades*
1856-58	Berlioz, *Les Troyens*
1904	Gilbert Murray's translation of *Trojan Women* published
1905	Murray's *Trojan Women* performed at Royal Court Theatre, London
1965	Sartre, *Les Troyennes* at Théâtre Nationale Populaire, Paris

Chronology

1971	Cacoyannis's film *Trojan Women* released
1974	First performance of Andrei Serban's *Trojan Women* as part of *Greek Trilogy*
1974	First performance of Tadashi Suzuki's *Toroia no Onna* (*Trojan Women*)
1983	*Trojan Women* produced at Habimah National Theatre, Tel Aviv, Israel
mid-1980s	Tony Harrison writes *Common Chorus I and II* (published 2002)
1993	Brendan Kennelly's *Trojan Women* published, and produced by the Abbey Theatre, Dublin
1995	*Trojan Women* directed by Annie Castledine in London
1996	Charles Mee's *Trojan Women 2.0: a love story* first produced in New York
1996	First performance of Ellen McLaughlin's *Trojan Women*
1997	First performance of Karen Hartman's *Troy Women*
1999	*Trojan Women* directed by JoAnne Akalaitis in Washington
2004	Femi Osofisan's *Women of Owu* first produced in Chipping Norton
2007	*Trojan Women* directed by Katie Mitchell in London

Index

Index